WILD WALKS

WILD WALKS
Sixty Short South Island Walks

Mark Pickering

Photographs by Nic Bishop
& Mark Pickering

SHOAL BAY PRESS

First published in 1995 by
Shoal Bay Press Ltd
Box 2151, Christchurch, New Zealand.

Revised edition published 1997

ISBN 0 908704 26 7

Cover photograph by Nic Bishop
Printed in Hong Kong through
Bookprint Consultants Ltd, Wellington

AUTHOR'S NOTE

Although I have visited all of these walks personally, I have gathered specific botanical and historical information from a wide variety of sources, including standard reference works, and the *Forest and Bird* and *New Zealand Geographic* magazines. Although every effort was made to have this book up to date with the most recent scientific research on New Zealand flora and fauna, it is a daunting task. Much intensive scientific study is being undertaken in all areas of the natural environment and some issues are controversial. Yesterday's plausible theory wilts under the attack of new hard data. Undoubtedly the next generation of researchers will produce some remarkable and quite unforeseen discoveries that will continue to enrich our appreciation of the wild things around us.

I want to acknowledge in particular the help of several pamphlets (many of which are now out of print),which established a good background for my own notes. To these mostly unnamed writers in the old Forest Service, Lands and Survey Department and the newer Department of Conservation, I express my thanks. Any errors are, of course, mine.

Several friends helped in the proofreading of the text and made many helpful suggestions. I wish to thank Nic Bishop, Jenny Brown, Barbara Brown and Dave Glenny. Nic also supplied many of the excellent wildlife photos, and Sven Brabyn helped considerably with computer expertise.

Mark Pickering

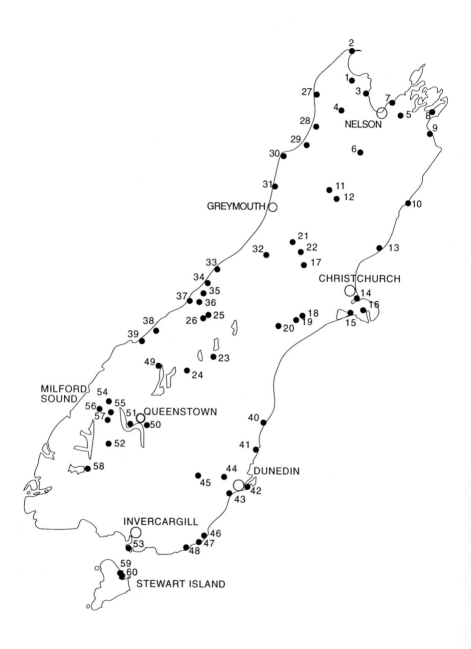

2

1

3

27

7

4

NELSON

5

8

28

9

29

6

30

31

11

12

GREYMOUTH

10

21

22

32

13

17

33

34

CHRISTCHURCH

35

14

37

16

36

25

26

18

38

19

39

20

15

23

49

24

MILFORD
SOUND

54

56

55

57

51

QUEENSTOWN

40

52

50

41

DUNEDIN

44

45

42

43

58

INVERCARGILL

46

47

53

48

59

60

STEWART ISLAND

CONTENTS

INTRODUCTION

These outstanding short walks in the South Island will guide you into the ancient magic of wilderness. The walks selected all have a landscape feature or wildlife habitat that makes them unique. The 'wild' in the title refers to the quality of landscape, not the difficulty in getting there. For some people the idea is a contradiction: surely if you can walk safely and easily to these places they can't really be wild? Not so!

New Zealand, and the South Island in particular, is blessed with wild places, and a good number of them are right under our noses. On a track such as Graves Walkway you can see fur seals and little blue penguins only 3km from the centre of Oamaru. Similar wilderness experiences can be enjoyed close to other urban areas, such as Scarborough Head near Christchurch, Sandfly Bay in Dunedin, and Boulder Bank near Nelson. Some of these walks you can virtually drive to, such as Ship Creek and Shag Point, but you miss the point if you stay in your car.

The South Island has a growing reputation for nature tourism, and something like a 'circuit' is developing for the keen do-it-yourself nature visitor. In many cases the best short walks are also the best for seeing New Zealand's unique wildlife and wild areas, and by combining walks and wildlife as a theme this book should appeal to a wide range of visitors to the South Island – whether home-bred New Zealanders or overseas tourists. Visitors touring the South Island in campervans will find this book particularly useful, as will backpackers with independent transport. It's hoped that even local people may be inspired to re-explore walks they took for granted.

Information

A good number of these walks have information boards on site. It is also worth trying your local Department of Conservation office (DOC) to see if it has pamphlets describing the walks in detail. There were quite a few available at one time or other, but many are now either out of print, or unavailable because they were produced by departments now extinct, such as the New Zealand Forest Service, or which now have no official interest in the area, such as the Department of Survey and Land Information (DOSLI, formerly the Lands and Survey Department). Even if DOC has not reprinted or revised the original pamphlet, it may well have inherited some of the old pamphlet stock.

There are several good field guide books for those interested in birds or plants. *Forest and Bird* magazine and *New Zealand Geographic* are highly recommended and contain many in-depth articles on wildlife and wild areas.

Maps

The maps printed in this book are a simple visual guide to the area and are not intended as a substitute for a topographical map. If you want to venture off the well-marked tracks you should be equipped with proper maps.

Guided wildlife tours

Throughout the South Island there are a number of commercial nature and wildlife tour operations. Some of these operations do not offer any more than an enterprising wildlife watcher could see on their own account, although they can be convenient for people short of time.

However, some commercial operators have exclusive access to unique wildlife that cannot be seen without joining their tour. The albatross colony at Taiaroa Head, the black petrels at Punakaiki, the white heron colony at Whataroa, and the whale-watching at Kaikoura are obvious examples. These commercial arrangements between the Department of Conservation and the tour operators are designed to control the management of a particular wildlife species better and reduce the stress on it.

The text will mention if there is a commercial operation for a unique species that cannot otherwise be easily seen. Some operations are seasonal and may be closed if there is no wildlife activity, or if the wildlife is sensitive to disturbance.

Features of the walks

• Each features some striking feature of landscape or wildlife.

• Many types of habitat are represented: estuaries, rainforest, granite gorges, tussock plains, coastal lagoons, limestone outcrops, hot springs – the works!

• Anyone from the elderly to young children can tackle these walks. No special equipment is needed, apart from a waterproof coat and strong shoes.

• The walks are generally easily accessible and well-graded, with information signs and often toilet facilities.

• None of the walks takes more than four hours (return).

Best time to go

All year round is the obvious answer, but people by and large prefer calm sunny days – naturally! Early morning and late evening are the most rewarding times for spotting wildlife, and a region that may bustle with activity then may by noon seem desolate. However, the more you come to study a particular area the more alive it seems: it's just a question of knowing where to look, and how.

Things to take

Good footwear, strong shoes or light boots, a parka, some food and maybe spare warm clothes during the winter months. Keep an eye on the weather, and on coastal walks keep an eye on the tides.

Binoculars are a marvellous asset for wildlife spotting, and alleviate the stress on birds and animals from people approaching too close for a better look.

Walking times

The walking times given here are conservative, and are designed to cater for slower walkers and families with young children. Any adult of reasonable fitness can reduce these times considerably.

Vandalism and graffiti
Because many of these walks are close to towns they periodically suffer from vandalism: people wreck signs, smash glass, shoot wildlife, etc. If you see the results of any of this behaviour please contact the local Department of Conservation office. If you actually *see* vandals in action, or some suspicious behaviour, take down the number plate of their car.

Sadly, some areas have become prone to graffiti, for example Tunnel Beach. It's true that in some historic areas Maori and European pioneers made similar personal graffiti, but since then we have multiplied alarmingly. While it may be interesting to see where one or two early travellers made a mark, it becomes ugly and meaningless when hundreds do so.

Mountain bikes
Mountain bikes are not permitted on most of these tracks. Even where no specific prohibition exists, mountain bikers should look elsewhere, as tyre tracks can cause serious ruts, and a speeding mountain bike is incompatible with a walker on a gentle stroll.

Wheelchair access
Although some of these tracks are suitable for wheelchairs, even on the best of them there can be obstacles such as bridges or tree roots that block progress. However, many of these walks start in visually interesting landscapes that are rewarding in their own right, so people with disabilities need not feel they have to venture far to see spectacular places and unique wildlife.

Closure of walks
A number of these walks may be closed for certain times of the year. This is particularly true in rural areas during the lambing months of August to November. Other reasons for closure may be fire risk or wildlife management. Please respect these closures.

TAKING CARE OF A WILD AREA
A few simple courtesies to the environment and to other users can keep these walks and their rightful inhabitants in their natural state.

Keep to the tracks
Please keep to the marked tracks. This is particularly important in fragile wetland areas.

Keep wildlife disturbance to a minimum
Some wild creatures, such as the harrier and weka, may seem to thrive on human presence, but this is not generally the case. Even the species mentioned suffer predation from dogs and shooting, or may be accidentally poisoned.

No feeding
The Department of Conservation discourages people from feeding friendly birds such as wekas and keas, tempting though it is to do so. Particularly in the case of keas it confirms them in their worst habits, disrupts their natural breeding cycles, and lures them away from their natural environment.

Injured wildlife
It is possible you will come across injured wildlife, particularly birds. However, remember these birds are *wild* and most have a nasty peck, and they may not take kindly to being rescued. Wild creatures may not even *need* rescuing, but may be simply resting, moulting, recovering from injuries or quietly dying. If in doubt it is better to seek expert advice – ring the local Department of Conservation.

In the case of stranded whales or injured seals, the Department of Conservation should be contacted at once. They have built up considerable expertise in these situations and can provide experienced advice for members of the public who wish to help out. The public can play an important part in the rescue of the larger sea mammals.

No dogs
Nearly all these walks have significant and easily disturbed wildlife, and people often do not realise how damaging dogs can be. They may not necessarily kill birds, or other wildlife, but continued disturbance, particularly at breeding times, can seriously interrupt breeding cycles, making it difficult for the birds to re-establish. Very often dog owners are themselves unaware of the consequences, and because they see no wildlife around think that it must be okay. If members of the public see uncontrolled dogs in inappropriate areas they should take it upon themselves to remind the dog owners politely of their obligations. There are plenty of other public spaces for exercising dogs.

No fires
This is an obvious safety measure: fires get out of control and disturb wildlife. In the case of coastal forests, the wood might not be as plentiful or as useless as it seems. Rotting wood provides good sites for insects, which in turn provide the food base for geckos and birds. Take a thermos and pre-cook your sausages.

No shooting
Of course! Although many of these walks shelter animals that may be legitimately shot, such as rabbits or possums, the close proximity of walkers makes uncontrolled shooting dangerous and illegal. Noxious animal control in these fragile areas is best left to the council or government bodies, which can manage a controlled shoot with minimal disturbance.

No rubbish
Leave only footprints, take only photos. Carry out other people's rubbish as well.

Collecting

This is a hard one, since it is the most natural thing in the world to pick a flower or collect an interesting stone. But think what you do with the items when you get home? The flower wilts, and the stone gets put on a shelf and after a while chucked out into the garden. Many of these walks are in fragile areas where if everyone grabbed a chunk of interesting material the consequences of degradation would be felt very quickly. People may think that their 'small bit' doesn't make a difference, but it does. We must learn to appreciate without possessing.

Food gathering

In the case of coastal areas with a vulnerable and unique habitat, the wildlife is usually more dependent on the food sources than you are. Shellfish beds can be depleted very quickly by people who invariably take more than they really need. In many cases the coastal walks do not explicitly forbid gathering of shellfish, but it is certainly good behaviour to leave the food chain intact.

Photography

All wildlife is vulnerable to disturbance at some point in its yearly cycle. A disturbed nest may be vulnerable to a predator, seals can be stampeded into the sea, and penguins can be trapped by their moulting feathers and may hurt themselves trying to escape.

Plenty of patience and skill is needed in wildlife photography, and the chances are that unless you have a few days to spare, good lenses and a tripod, you are unlikely to come away with a particularly good photo – and you may have unnecessarily disturbed the wildlife into the bargain. The human eye is the best lens, along with a good pair of binoculars.

WILDLIFE CODE OF CONDUCT

1. If you see a wild creature keep a reasonable distance.
2. If chicks or young animals are present, be especially discreet. Remember, the parents only need to be absent from their eggs for a few minutes to seriously affect the chances of those eggs hatching. And predators are always on the lookout for unattended young.
3. Be patient.
4. Approach slowly, avoid sudden movements and loud noises, and wherever possible reduce your profile.
5. Do not come between them and their escape route (for example, seals and the sea).
6. Do not feed.
7. Get expert help for the 'rescue' of injured wildlife.
8. Most birds and animals give warning signals or movements if they feel uncomfortable. Respect their space and withdraw.

NELSON

The crystal-clear Pupu Springs

WAIKOROPUPU SPRINGS

Features
Natural freshwater spring and plants, historic gold workings.

Walking time
30 minutes return.

How to get there
From Highway 60, about 4km north of Takaka, turn left after the Waitapu Bridge and drive 4 kilometres to the Waikoropupu (more commonly known as Pupu) Springs carpark, toilet and information boards.

This is the largest freshwater natural spring in New Zealand and has been dubbed 'a submerged Garden of Eden'. It bubbles up from aquifers (underground water channels and levels) flowing through the limestone rocks that occupy a good deal of the Takaka Valley. A mudstone 'cap' overlays the limestone generally, but at Pupu Springs the cap has been eroded, allowing the aquifer water to force its way up to the surface.

The walk is an easy 30-minute circuit following boardwalks to various points of interest. A goldmining operation earlier this century has left a network of sluice channels and water races criss-crossing the springs reserve,

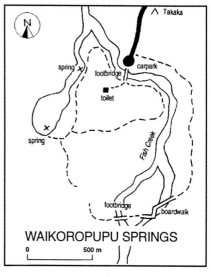

with a number of impressive hand-stacked tailings. A shrub forest in the form of tall manuka, gorse and young rimu now covers the reserve.

The track first skirts a small spring, then reaches the main spring. The flow ranges from 7 to 21 cubic metres per second (cumecs) at a constant temperature of 11.7 °C. The water has spent some three to four years underground – chilled, crystal-clear, like a perfect natural wine.

The underwater plants are a swathe of mosses, algae, liverworts, milfoil, water forget-me-not, duckweed and submerged cress, swaying in the watery breeze. There are also koura (freshwater crayfish). Slight tides have been measured in the springs, possibly caused by 'earth tides', the flexing of the earth rather than the movement of the seas. There is a very slight salt taint, 0.5 per cent, caught from seawater intruding into the aquifers. There are several undersea natural springs recorded in Golden Bay.

Features

Sandspit, wading and migrant birds, sand patterns, manuka forest.

Walking time

To Fossil Point 1 hour return; Fossil Point circuit 1 hour return; Old Man Peak 2 hours return. Remember, this is a working farm park, and care should be taken not to disturb stock. Walks may be closed during lambing in September/October.

How to get there

From Collingwood in Golden Bay take the Pakawau and Port Puponga road for 25km. Just 1km past Port Puponga are the visitor centre, cafe, toilets, viewing telescope, information boards and carpark. On a fine day you can see Mount Taranaki, 144km away, from the hilltop behind the centre. The cafe is closed in winter.

On a large-scale map of New Zealand, Farewell Spit looks like a giant kiwi's beak, curving for 30km and enclosing Golden Bay. It is a unique feature formed by conflicting currents, and it is uninhabited, windswept and wild. For migratory birds it is a marvellous summer resting place. The spit has been designated a wetland of international importance, and upwards of a hundred different bird species have been recorded here. Public walking access is restricted to the base of the spit, but a four-wheel-drive tourist venture based in Collingwood runs tours along the spit to the lighthouse.

The best short walk starts from the carpark and follows the inland curve of the spit, until it picks up a vehicle track and crosses through the dry manuka forest to the windswept sands by the Tasman Sea. There are interesting rock shapes and tidal platforms at Fossil Point, so it pays to try to go at low tide.

In geological terms the spit is a consequence of debris flowing out of the West Coast rivers: the lighter sands are carried by currents along to the top of the South Island. Here the current pattern becomes more complex but one branch turns into the shallow enclave of Golden Bay dragging its 'tail' of sand behind. The spit appears

---

WHALE STRANDINGS

Whale strandings are an unfortunate feature of the spit (note the sperm whale jawbone at the carpark) and these occurrences are still not well understood. Pilot whales in particular get caught here, but sperm, minke and fin whales have all been included in the bizarre death toll. In New Zealand whale strandings have tended to occur in estuarine or gently shelving waters, where perhaps the mammals get confused by the subtle profile of a 'gentle' shore in comparison to one with clearly defined features, such as headlands and cliffs. All the strandings on Farewell Spit have been on the inside of the spit, in Golden Bay itself, which is a large shallow bay with few prominent coastal features.

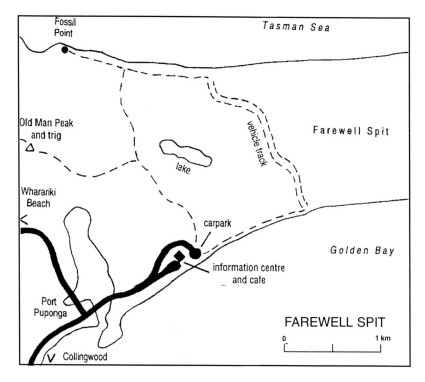

Fossil Point

Tasman Sea

Old Man Peak and trig

Farewell Spit

vehicle track

lake

Wharariki Beach

carpark

information centre and cafe

Golden Bay

Port Puponga

FAREWELL SPIT

0   1 km

Collingwood

to be widening rather than lengthening, some 3.4 million cubic metres of material being deposited each year.

There is extensive evidence of Maori occupation and the original vegetation of the spit has been modified several times. It is likely that the spit once supported a broadleaf coastal forest – akeake, ngaio, mahoe etc – with perhaps some pockets of karaka, totara, rimu and kahikatea. European grazing rights and fires demolished most of this vegetation and today the dominant plants are marram grass, lupin and pasture grasses, with only limited stands of manuka and isolated cabbage trees. The large swamp areas hold rushes and flax.

It is the extensive network of tidal wetlands that provides an immense food source, making the spit so important for birdlife. The sheer number of birds is hard to grasp: up to 20,000 bar-tailed godwits and 25,000 lesser knots (both nest in Siberia, some 12,000 kilometres away!) and many other wading species with such curious names as the Mongolian dotterel, wrybill, little whimbrel, grey-tailed tattler, banded dotterel and turnstone.

These birds live according to the tides: as the mudplain is exposed by the falling tide the birds flock to feed; as the tide comes in they retreat to roost. The mass migration in autumn is one of the most extraordinary wildlife sights in New Zealand, rarely witnessed, as the waders head back for the defrosting spring conditions of the tundra, leaving a scattering of wintering-over birds.

NIC BISHOP

South Island pied oystercatchers

Apart from the waders, other spit birds include the sparrow, royal spoonbill, kea, weka, chaffinch, song thrush, pipit, skylark, yellowhammer, skua, oyster-catcher, paradise duck, gannet (now nesting on the sand and shell banks) and the ubiquitous black swan.

The 'presence' of the spit is powerful, and has not been better expressed than by an unnamed poet in a pamphlet issued by the Department of Lands and Survey:

The spit is a savage place; high winds sweep curtains of stinging sand along the wide, glaring beaches and howl off the tops of the dunes, whose flowing sand pours like drifting snow across the landscape. During lulls the sand may settle in beautifully moulded ripples across the dunes, but elsewhere, when the wind has gone, dunes may have been stripped by flying sand to reveal an intricate pattern of dark (heavy) and lighter layers, looking for all the world like old burnished wood-grain. A breeze picks up; here and there the grains become active and hop about fitfully. The wind increases (80 kilometres an hour is not unusual) and scurries of sand begin to move across the beaches. At full gale nothing is visible except a fog of scalding sand as the dunes' crests melt down and the beach becomes uninhabitable. Little wonder that each strand-line and em-bayment contains driftwood jewels, shaped and smoothed by the abrasive wind.'

MARAHAU ESTUARY

Features
Estuary flats, saltmarsh, sand coves, coastal forest.

Walking time
About 2-3 hours exploring the estuary, Tinline Nature Walk and returning by the bush track. Take care: a low tide is obviously essential and the tide can come in with surprising speed.

How to get there
From Motueka drive north 5km to the Kaiteriteri turn-off, then 8km to the Marahau carpark, toilets, information shelter and cafe.

This walk is a cruisy way to get the feel of the Abel Tasman National Park, with its huge low-tide estuarine habitat and lingering sand coves, the sculpted rocks, the crystal-clear water, the dry rustling forest, the unexpected wildlife. With sandshoes that you do not mind getting wet or salty, this estuary is an easy and revealing place to explore and, combined with a diversion into the lush podocarps of the Tinline Nature Walk, makes for a pleasing contrast of habitats.

From the Marahau carpark at low tide you can step off the causeway onto the firm sands and a 'meadow' of salt-tolerant glasswort, which grows like a miniature forest along the shoreline. Morning sun brings out the subtle and intricate range of colours, through many shades of red to orange and purple tones – a true tapestry of the sea.

Estuaries can look unimpressive and empty from a distance, but they are in fact one of the most productive of natural habitats. The mud is full of shellfish, worms and crustaceans. Wading birds feed on this abundance: some like the white-faced heron stabbing at their prey with sharp beaks, others like the curlews scooping their beaks through the water. Oystercatchers make a noisy chatter when you approach, and there are pied stilts and godwits. Welcome swallows flit over the sand-flats, and on the margins it's quite common to see familiar birds such as sparrows and thrushes chasing the insects that breed in the mounds of rotting seaweed.

Just before the first headland is a small cove called Tinline Bay with a rock island, its flanks sculpted by wave action. Around the headland is Coquille Bay, a pretty stretch of sand. It would involve a bit of clambering to get further around the rocks at low tide past Guilbert Point to Appletree Bay, so it's easiest to return to

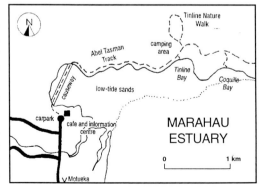

NIC BISHOP

Common mud crab

Marahau by following the marked track up through a shady gully cluttered with kiekie vines and ferns to the main Abel Tasman Track. This is well graded and passes a good lookout point before descending to a sheltered open clearing with picnic tables and a toilet.

The Tinline Nature Walk is signposted from here, and there are two short loop tracks signposted with official irony:

1. 'The bush as it was' (20 minutes);
2. 'After the fire' (10 minutes).

The 'bush as it was' is a lovely mix of silver beech, black beech, hard beech, rimu, matai, a rare totara and kahikatea, with a dense second storey of pepper tree, lancewood, toro and numerous other native species and a mat of ferns and lichens underneath. The 'after the fire' walk shows the damage fire causes, and the success of the radiata pine that seeded itself in the ash ruins of the native trees. In the long term the native species will re-establish themselves, denying light to the seedlings of the ageing pine trees.

Back on the main track it is an easy stroll to Marahau. The original vegetation was all burnt off and the resulting regrowth is a horrible and competitive mix of manuka, pine tree, akeake, gorse, broom, bracken, toro and native ferns, all fighting it out for space and light. Eventually the native trees will win, but it's interesting to note that this regenerating forest supports a healthy population of birds – bellbirds, song thrushes, blackbirds, silvereyes and chaffinches, all of which are vocal and easily seen.

At Marahau the tide is returning quickly, pushing in the algae-rich water that acts as a life-blood to the estuary's plants and animals.

FLORA TABLELAND

Features
Beech forest, bush birds, alpine tussock, rock shelters, limestone formations, historic pack track.

Walking time
Grid Iron Gulch 3 hours return, Salisbury Hut 4-5 hours return. Please note that this is alpine country and snow can fall throughout the year.

How to get there
On Highway 61 between Motueka and Kohatu drive to Ngatimoti (19km from Motueka) and follow the signs to the Graham Valley and Mount Arthur. Just as the Flora road starts to climb it becomes very steep and smaller, front-wheel-drive cars may have difficulty with traction here, particularly after rain when the shingle mixes with mud and becomes greasy, and some of the bedrock is exposed. After this point the road is stable, but it is still steep, and it is a long climb to the carpark at 900m.

Once you get there you are rewarded with a superb view looking back to Nelson. There are also information boards, an intentions book and a toilet.

It is rare in New Zealand to reach an area of alpine bush with such a wealth of walking opportunities, and it would take several trips to explore the beauties of this landscape.

History is entwined through the forest, for it is the old goldminers' trail from Nelson to Takaka that has effectively opened up the region for modern walkers. The early explorers faced a bewildering landscape, the bush plateau riven with deep streams and karst limestone fissures. They made temporary homes under the limestone overhangs, probably caught wekas, cooked them over fires, scratched their names into the rock and passed on.

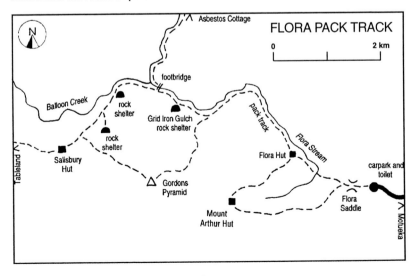

FLORA PACK TRACK

0   2 km

THE CHAFFEYS OF ASBESTOS COTTAGE

Theirs is an extraordinary story. It's easy to visit the wilderness, but can you imagine living there? Henry and Annie Chaffey did just that for 40 years, moving to their mountain hideaway hut, now known as Asbestos Cottage, in about 1915. Both came from unsuccessful and difficult first marriages, and only formally tied the knot in 1932 when Annie's first husband died.

Henry was a prospector, of tidy, natty appearance, who loved to explore the mountains and bush and left Annie for long periods alone. Annie was always dressed the lady and left the mountains only once in her 39-year sojourn. She was adaptable, made all her own clothes (in a staunchly Victorian style), bottled jam, – even saw 80 jars get destroyed in the devastating 1929 Murchison earthquake. In 1941 she was given an orange – the first she had seen for 28 years!

Henry Chaffey died of a heart attack in 1951, aged 83. Annie lived for two unhappy years in Timaru, dying at 75. The cottage still stands and is maintained as a Department of Conservation hut.

Once you've enjoyed the view from the carpark, and the attentions of those friendly fiends the keas, walk along the broad track that climbs to the Flora Saddle. Here a side-track goes up to Mount Arthur Hut, and another track leaves that hut and goes down to Flora Hut – so you can complete a circuit. But the main trail follows a gentle grade down to the old Flora Hut with its twin huts sharing a common porch.

The pack track now follows the Flora Stream, and it is a very soothing walk through the subtly shaded beech forest, across various footbridges to the spectacular rock overhangs at Grid Iron Gulch. The bivvy rocks have been enlarged somewhat and a drip-line added, and various domestic features have been built in, such as a fireplace, swing chair and bunks. In case you missed it, just before the main rocks a trail zigzags steeply up the slope to another natural overhang, with a fireplace and a snug hut with its own glass murals. Quite a work of art.

From Grid Iron Gulch it's only another 15 minutes to a track junction and then the track turns up Balloon Creek and passes the tiny Growler Rock Shelter, eventually passing another side-trail leading to another rock shelter (an historic site, for many old names have been carved on the rock walls) and onto the tussock Tableland. From here it is 30 minutes to Salisbury Hut, which has a superb view of the Arthur Range and the fierce-looking Twins.

If you have time there is some interesting karst landscape on the track to Gordon's Pyramid: sinkholes, limestone outcrops and that strange rustling silence so characteristic of dry karst areas.

PELORUS BRIDGE

Features
Beech forest, river pools, bush birds.

Walking time
Totara Walk 30 minutes return; Circle Walk 30 minutes return; Tawa Walk 30 minutes return.

How to get there
On Highway 6 drive 18km from Havelock. Camping ground, camping area, tearooms, picnic areas, carpark and toilets. The tearooms are popular, and it is wonderfully decadent to sit outside enjoying good coffee while you listen to the native birds.

Where the Pelorus River passes underneath the skeletal steel bridge of Highway 6, it lingers and settles in deep azure pools, where fine fat trout move sluggishly between the sculpted rocks. The water is stunningly clear and it's hard to resist the temptation to sample it. Dense beech forest, mingled with podocarps such as rimu and kahikatea, spreads across both sides of the highway and there is a refreshingly solid chorus of native birdsong.

There are over 230 native plant species recorded in the reserve, and you can wander off down any of the tracks for a look at the impressive trees occupying this fertile valley floor. Black beech and hard beech dominate, with rimu, matai, miro and kahikatea poking through the beech canopy. Underneath the forest is thick with second-storey plants such as the spikey juvenile lancewood, hinau, mingimingi, kamahi and pigeonwood. Mosses, lichens and ferns fill up the ground-floor spaces.

For a quick look you can drive to the Kahikatea Flat, where clean-limbed kahikateas provide a lovely shape against the sky, and you can hear the bright clear notes of bellbirds and tuis echoing in the grassy glade. Kaka also visit. The wood pigeon is easier to spot as it 'whooshes' through the forest canopy. Kereru have been specially studied here, and it's been noted that they feed mostly on leaves from August to December, and then on fruit from December onwards.

Pelorus Bridge

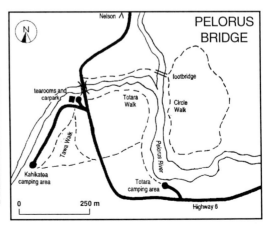

WASPS

New Zealand has several types of wasp. Its own native species go relatively unnoticed but the introduced German wasp and common wasp are much more aggressive.

These wasps are ferocious and highly competitive, attacking almost any other insect, chicks in nests and, of course, humans. In some areas, notably Pelorus Bridge, where the honeydew in the beech forest is a major attraction, the wasps once reached almost plague proportions, with an enormous and still largely not understood effect on the native bird and insect populations.

NIC BISHOP

The common wasp queen usually hibernates in winter, then lays worker eggs that feed her as she lays new queen eggs and drone eggs. These hatch and mate and the new queens form nests of their own. A wasp nest usually houses about 400-500 wasps.

Cold conditions usually kill off all except the queen, though in warmer areas the nest survives and can grow to an abnormal size. While harsh winters can help reduce the size of the colonies, the wasps themselves sometimes have such an explosive population growth that they outgrow their food source and suffer a population crash.

Humans have introduced natural parasites that live on wasp nests, and one of the most successful introductions has been in the Pelorus area. But this process is slow and on its own insufficient. The reality is that wasps will continue to be a permanent feature of our landscape, particularly beech forest, and, as with so much of our flora and fauna, humans have to find (usually expensive) ways to manage what we have accidentally introduced.

HONEYDEW

Black beech often has a sooty-looking fungus growing on its trunk, which grows on the secretions of a scale insect feeding on sap under the bark. You can see the tiny white 'anal tube' threads of the insect and often spot the sweet-tasting drops dangling at the end. Honey-eaters such as the tui, bellbird and silvereye enjoy this bounty, as do bees, which gather the secretions and turn them into honeydew, which has itself become a useful export crop. Insects that live in the sooty fungus also provide a food source for the birds. You can smell the heady honeydew scent in season, but unfortunately it also attracts wasps.

LAKE ROTOITI

Features
Alpine lake, mountain views, beech forest, bush birds.

Walking time
Two hours.

How to get there
On Highway 63 between Blenheim and Kawatiri Junction drive to St Arnaud then a further kilometre to the road end where there's a shelter, campsites, picnic areas, extensive walks, visitor centre and toilets.

At 800m altitude the air of Lake Rotoiti is crisp and clean. This lake is one of the two (the other is Rotoroa) that form the northern boundary of the Nelson Lakes National Park, which now stretches all the way to Lewis Pass Scenic Reserve. This extensive mountain area provides the catchments that give birth to some of the South Island's great rivers, including the Clarence, the Waiau, the Wairau and the Buller, which begins its journey from Lake Rotoiti itself.

This walk strolls through dense attractive beech forest and back along the edge of Lake Rotoiti. From the carpark at Kerrs Bay you can follow the Lakeside Track for an hour to the signposted Loop Track junction, then walk back along the lake foreshore on the gravel bank. There are several seats by the shoreline.

The main beech species by the lakeside are red, silver and black. Red beech is distinguished by its large size and tall reddish trunk. There are some good specimens

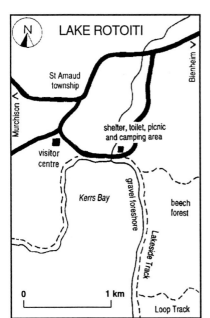

here, some with massively buttressed roots. Silver beech has smaller leaves, toothed like red beech, and black beech has smaller leaves still, but not fretted and coming to a rounded point.

Underneath this canopy are several dominant understorey plants that can survive in the low light conditions, such as putaputaweta, lancewood, kamahi and kohuhu. At ground level you find ferns, mosses, liverworts, fungi and orchids (best seen in spring and summer on moss-covered logs and beside small streams). Lichens often cover the lower trunks and branches of the beech, and after rain can absorb up to five times their body weight in water, usually changing colour from their drier brown-yellows to green. A distinctive lichen is the wispy hanging white-green old man's beard or maidenhair, which dangles from branches.

25

FUNGI

Fungi exert a fascination for humans. They are neither vegetable nor animal but occupy a separate taxonomic kingdom of their own. They have secretive lives: popping up unexpectedly, disappearing abruptly. They can smell awful, look repulsive, and yet demonstrate some of the most vivid dashes of colour in the forest. We are allowed to eat some fungi, but are forbidden to eat others. It is now believed that the world's largest single living organism is a fungus, a species of Armillaria, covering 600 hectares underground in the Cascade Mountains, Washington State.

Fungi are a huge kingdom and in this forest walk you can see several different types. Root fungi associate themselves with the roots of beech trees and other plants. Their mycelium (or network of feeding threads) is, like an iceberg, mostly hidden and represents the bulk of the organism. The visible and brightly coloured fungus top, which is the fruiting body, lives for only a short period.

The black sooty mould that grows on black beech trees in particular is a type of fungus. It feeds on the secretions from the honeydew scale insect, which itself lives off the tree.

Bracket fungi (right) grow on the beech trunks and can be obviously identified by their shape. The 'brackets' are hard, usually white underneath and brown on top.

Strawberry fungus

Silver beech trees support a unique 'strawberry' fungus, as it is often called. The honeycomb balls develop on the branches and can often be seen in their hundreds, fallen to the base of trees, where they are eaten by insects and birds.

Lake Rotoiti

The honeydew from the scale insects that bury into the trunks of beech trees is an important source of food for the nectar-eaters such as bellbirds and tuis – you are bound to hear them. These birds also feed on such insects as dragonflies and cicadas. Other native birds are the grey warbler, yellow-breasted tomtit, rifleman and kaka. This bush parrot tears off the bark of trees to get at the larvae of wood-boring insects, and sometimes you can see small piles of wood chips at the base of a tree. Non-native birds include the blackbird and song thrush.

At the lake edge mallards are common, as well as grey ducks. Both the pied shag and black shag can often be spotted resting on the lake shore. Brown trout have been introduced to the lake waters, and there are long-finned eels and freshwater mussels as well.

BOULDER BANKS

Features
Boulder banks, estuary and salt meadows, shore birds.

How to get there
Drive 4km from Nelson on Highway 6 and turn into the Whakapuaka Reserve on Boulder Bank Drive. This short road has the estuary on one side and the wildlife reserve, pony club and oxidation ponds on the other. It is another 1km to the sea and boulder bank.

For the Delaware Inlet boulder bank drive 14km on Highway 6 to Hira, then turn onto Cable Bay Road and drive 6km to the carpark on top of the bank.

Nelson Haven, Boulder Bank & Whakapuaka Wildlife Reserve

Boulder banks are very odd geographical features, and there are two of them in the Nelson region, both formed in the same manner and both creating estuary habitats that abound with wildlife.

The Nelson boulder bank is by the far the longest at 13km, and encloses the Nelson Haven estuary, at the east end of which is the Whakapuaka Reserve. The hard igneous boulders were eroded from McKay Bluff to the east and rolled by the southwest drift of tides and currents to form this curious natural feature, which is still being accumulated. There's an historic lighthouse at the end of the bank, built of cast iron in England and shipped out to New Zealand in sections. It was commissioned in 1862 and stands 20m high.

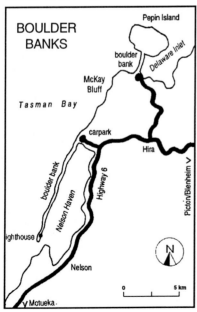

The bank itself is hardly easy walking, with its loose stones and pebbles, but from the Whakapuaka Reserve you get a good idea of its character. There are over a thousand black-backed gulls' nests on the bank in summer, and small colonies of oystercatchers, red-billed gulls and white-fronted terns (tara). The Maori knew the bank as 'whakatu', which has been translated as the 'place where the broken canoes were piled'.

The various uses of the Whakapuaka Reserve might seem contradictory – it is host to a model plane area, a pony club and land yachting as well as being a wildlife reserve – but the bird populations look healthy. The oxidation ponds support a busy population of mallards, pied stilts, red-billed gulls and paradise ducks, and the side-channels that run through the reserve are lined with the subtle and suggestive colours of the marsh glasswort. There are usually white-faced herons probing the shallows. Harriers often circle the marsh area, and kingfishers make flashy appearances with their distinctive *kek-kek* call.

Delaware Inlet & Boulder Bank
The Delaware Inlet, with its tidal mudflats, salt meadows and saltmarshes, has been formed between two unusual features – a boulder bank at Cable Bay and a sandspit or tombola at Delaware Bay. The boulder bank has completely closed the gap between Pepin Island and the mainland, with the material source coming from a bluff on Pepin Island.

The estuary is a complex structure. The mudflats at low tide host large numbers of mud crabs and snails, as well as shellfish such as pipis, cockles, whelks and small black mussels. On the intertidal zone the typical plant is eelgrass (sometimes mistaken for a seaweed), which with its dense root network is well adapted to this fickle and harsh environment.

Sea lettuce can be a seasonally abundant algae, with its distinctive and bright green paper-thin sheets. In the saltmarsh areas plants such as raupo (bullrush), club rush, umbrella sedge, saltwater ribbonwood and the attractive jointed wire rush have to withstand short inundations of seawater. Salt meadows on the very fringes of the saline belt often have mat-forming plants such as shore pimpernel, with its charming white flowers in spring, and button-weed, with yellow daisy-like flowers in mid-summer. Harakeke, the native flax,

Boulder bank, Delaware inlet

29

NIC BISHOP

White-faced heron

has also established communities around the shoreline, which attract nectar-feeding birds such as tuis and bellbirds.

Birdlife is abundant and over 30 species have been recorded here. Little blue penguins probably breed on Pepin Island and the Delaware spit, and the black shag and little shag feed around the estuary, as does the easily identified white-faced heron. Black swans, paradise shelducks, mallards, some grey ducks, pukeko, oystercatchers, banded dotterels (which breed on Delaware spit) and the three gull species can all be seen at various times of the year. Three tern species have been noted but you are most likely to see the white-fronted, skimming and diving at high speed for small fish. Kingfishers and swallows haunt the estuary margins, and the New Zealand pipit may be seen too.

Plenty of fish species visit the estuary at full tides. Typical are the eagleray, stingray, pilchard, whitebait, trevally, kahawai, jack mackerel, sand flounder, yellow-eyed mullet and both species of eel.

There is a walkway linking Cable Bay (the site of a telegraph link established in 1876) and the Glen carpark some 2-3 hours one way along the coast. It's a stiff climb up the hill, but the reward is excellent views over Delaware Inlet and the coast west towards Nelson.

MARLBOROUGH SOUNDS & KAIKOURA

KARAKA POINT – TE RAE O KARAKA

Features
Bush peninsula and beaches, Maori pa site, drowned valleys.

How to get there
From Picton take the Waikawa Road some 8km to the large carpark area.

Walking time
30 minutes return.

This short peninsula once housed a Maori pa, bustling with human activity. Amid the preparing of food, fishing, and repairs to huts and the palisade walls any sighting of a craft in the empty sounds would be sure to arouse interest. Nowadays the situation is reversed. The pa site is quiet, but Queen Charlotte Sound is the busiest waterway in the sounds, with dozens of pleasure craft arriving and departing from Picton each day, trying to dodge the big surge of water from the frequent passage of the Cook Strait ferries.

Some remains of the pa site can still be identified. There is a ditch and bank across the narrowest point of the peninsula, which would have had a palisade on top. Beyond there are several large pits, some of which might have been used for kumara (sweet potato). Here and there the piles of broken shells reveal rubbish pits or middens.

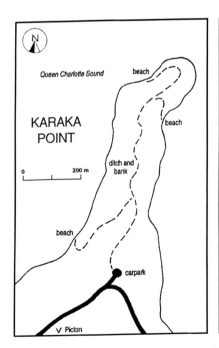

MAORI PA

Pa were fortified Maori villages and pa sites abound throughout New Zealand. A site such as Karaka would be typical in being well positioned, both for food-gathering (shellfish and saltwater fish) and as a lookout for rival tribes. A good defensive structure was imperative, so a pa was invariably sited where at least some sides were difficult to approach. Outside the pa site there would have been kumara fields, bird-snaring areas and drying racks for fish and eels, and the Maori inhabitants would have retreated to the defended pa when a threat developed. Water was always a difficulty for many pa sites such as Karaka, which relied on a water source outside the palisade walls.

View from the carpark over the Sounds

From the carpark the track drops down into the predominantly manuka bush, with karo (pittosporum), akeake, koromiko and broadleaf underneath and on the edge of the glades. On the rocky edges gorse and broom secure a niche. Bellbirds can become vocal above the introduced chatter of sparrows and song thrushes.

The Marlborough Sounds themselves are not glacial-carved, like fiords, but rather are drowned valleys, where the land has tilted and the sea invaded, creating a complexity of channels and inlets.

There are several short side-tracks that lead down to tiny sand beaches and some decent afternoon sunbathing by the lapping waters.

WAIRAU LAGOON

Features
Wildlife lagoon, saltmarsh, moa-hunter
information site.

Walking time
3-4 hours circuit. No water.

How to get there
From Blenheim drive 5km south on
Highway 1 to Hardings Road, and 1km to
the carpark.

Over 6000 years ago gravels from the Awatere River pushed into Cloudy Bay and, because of the northern currents, gradually formed a boulder bank over 7km long. The water from the Wairau River and other streams 'pooled' behind this obstacle and formed a complex lagoon wetland.

Wetlands are rich and dynamic and, despite first appearances, generally contain the greatest diversity of animal and plant life of any habit on earth. Biologically they are productive and usually provide crucial spawning and nursery grounds for many fish species. The warm and shallow metre-deep waters of the Wairau are home to spotties, black flounders and kahawai. The smaller fish in turn provide food for diving birds such as pied shags and terns. The mudflats are home to juvenile fish, shellfish and worms, which typically attract oystercatchers, pied stilts and godwits. Black swans are fond of the saltmarsh and reedy zones, and in the dry silt fringes of the lagoons you get many common insect feeders such as fantails, pipits and finches. Over 70 bird species have been recorded here, including nesting royal spoonbills.

At the carpark you are reminded of the sea's influence by the presence of the salt-tolerant glasswort (nicknamed sea asparagus for its looks, not its taste), which is the dominant plant on this walking track. It forms a virtual miniature forest beside the tidal waterways, blending into dozens of subtle colour shades.

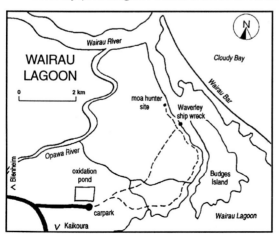

Past the information board the track divides and the left fork crosses side-channels and wanders along the fringe of the estuary. A pair of binoculars is very useful for bird-spotting, because the raucous red-billed gulls keep up a clamour overhead at your intrusion and scare off most of the other species.

After an hour you reach the beached wreck

of the *Waverley*, 30m long and built in 1883. It was scuttled and later pushed by a flood up this side-channel, where it provides a convenient lookout post for gulls and sunning site for shags. There's even a shrub living inside it.

A side-trail goes 20 minutes to a view of the Wairau Bar and information boards that tell the story of the first humans who were attracted to the lagoon. About 1000

Wreck of the Waverley

years ago Maori moa-hunters lived in camps around the lagoon, catching small moas, manufacturing stone tools, and constructing canals in the wetland to trap moulting birds and eels. European settlement began on the Wairau Bar in 1847, when an inn was built to cater for the coastal trading ships that used the 'port' of Wairau and also had access up the Opawa River to 'Beaver', the unlikely name at the time for Blenheim. A small fishing community still exists by the Wairau Lagoon.

The return trail cuts across the flat marsh meadows, where midges and flies can sometimes swarm in unpleasant numbers, and a harrier hawk may wheel slowly overhead. In late evening the colours in the marsh sedge turn into an embroidery of reds and purples.

MOAS

Moas were ratites – flightless birds – like the kiwi. There were 11 species of moa living in a wide range of habitats including grasslands, forests and the sub-alpine environment. Because of the absence of any large browsing mammals in New Zealand, moas seemed to occupy this niche, with some species growing to a considerable size – 2m high and weighing up to 250kg. Other bush and alpine moas were much smaller, around 15-20kg – more like a turkey or swan.

The discovery of moa remains with Maori remains on the Wairau Bar in 1939 told us a lot about the moa-hunter culture. An extinct giant eagle (with a 3m wingspan) preyed on the moa, but it was the arrival of the Maori that destroyed the big birds. Fire spread by humans eliminated much of their habitat and the birds were obviously a valuable food source. By the 17th century, about 700 years after the first Polynesians arrived, the moa was all but extinct. There is a Maori lament and saying: 'Ka ngaro i te ngaro a te moa' – 'lost as the moa is lost'.

KAIKOURA PENINSULA

Features

Fur seals, nesting seagulls, tidal platform.

Walking time

Full circuit shoreline and clifftop walk circuit 4-5 hours, if using the Whalers Bay track 3 hours. Note the Shoreline Walk is a low-tide route only and gulls can dive-bomb you during spring.

How to get there

Turn off Highway 1 and drive through the Kaikoura township to Fyffe Quay and Point Kean carpark at the far end, where there are information boards, shelter and barbecue sites. Toilets 1km before the carpark. Access can also be gained on the other side of the peninsula, down South Bay Parade to the carpark and recreation area.

Excellent views and excellent wildlife on this walkway around the tip of the Kaikoura Peninsula, which juts out into the 1000m-deep waters of an oceanic canyon that attracts deep-feeding mammals such as sperm and southern right whales. At high tide at Point Kean seals like to bask on rocks barely 20m away from the parked cars, and in general the wildlife here is approachable, if wary.

Over 12,000 red-billed gulls (tarapunga) nest at several sites around the peninsula, collectively the largest colony in the South Island. There are smaller colonies of black-billed gulls and about 4000 white-fronted terns (tara). The terns can be identified by their black caps and their rapid flitting over the waves, which has earned them the delightful nickname 'sea-swallow'. The spring breeding season is clamorous with activity, and the gulls in particular can be aggressive towards intruders.

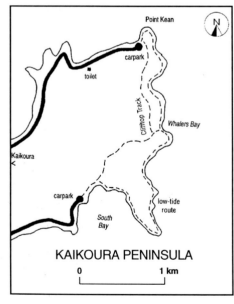

KAIKOURA PENINSULA

0   1 km

What attracts this multifarious wildlife is the mingling of warm northerly currents with colder subantarctic currents, causing an explosive growth of plankton-like organisms that encourage fish, and in turn seals and other mammals such as the Hector's dolphin and the acrobatic Dusky dolphin. The legendary orca is also drawn to this wildlife wealth, not to mention the famous Kaikoura crayfish.

From the carpark at low tide it is easy walking on the micro-landscape of the limestone and mudstone tidal platforms. As well as shellfish and bull kelp there are many wading and shore birds: banded dotterels, oystercatchers, turnstones, gannets, reef heron, white-faced heron, shearwaters, and pied and black shags. More surprisingly, you can spot mallard and paradise ducks feeding and paddling in the tide pools. Little blue penguins also come ashore here.

The seals are always highly visible and easy to smell, with several mostly non-breeding colonies established along the coastline. These are mostly males, with up to 500 present during the winter season. Pups are often seen, some of which may have been born here, though usually they have arrived from breeding colonies further south. Each year the colonies grow larger and visitors should take care as they scramble among the rocks – it's quite easy to step on a dozing seal. Make sure you do not come between the seals and their escape route to the sea.

Red-billed gulls

Before Whalers Bay there is a side-track that links up with the Clifftop Track. Many people prefer to climb up here and return to Point Kean. At Whalers Bay there is a signposted cave, guarded by mahoe trees and ongaonga (stinging nettle), then several brilliantly white sea-stacks patterned in a characteristic 'platey' shapes.

There are more tidal platforms before you turn the finger-like promontory of Atia Point (Shark's Tooth), and then attractive tidal pools and platforms around to the South Bay carpark and reserve.

Once you've walked along the shoreline it's worth going back via the Clifftop Track – the views are grand.

Humans were the last and most effective predator attracted to the Kaikoura Peninsula, in fact Kaikoura means 'crayfish food'.

The Maori occupied the peninsula for hundreds of years with over 14 known pa sites. Then came the Europeans in the 1840s in pursuit of the whales, until in the 1920s the supply was exhausted. Ironically, it is this same beast that is responsible for Kaikoura's current 'boom': whale-watching is one of the most popular tourist adventures in the South Island.

Striking linear patterns in the tidal platform

WHALE-WATCHING
These guided tours operate all year round and use echo-location equipment to track the whales, particularly the impressive sperm whales, when they surface. The tours usually see Hector's dolphins and visit the fur seal colony. The Kaikoura information centre has details.

LEWIS PASS

Clematis — puawananga

LAKE DANIELLS

Features
Red beech forest, alpine lake, bush birds, kaka.

Walking time
Five minutes to the Sluice Box Gorge, 3-4 hours return to Lake Daniells.

How to get there
On Highway 7 the Lake Daniells turnoff is 5km east of Springs Junction at the Marble Hill picnic area. Camping area and toilets.

From a layperson's point of view there are two general types of forest in the South Island. The first is the wet, luxuriant jungle-like rainforest, dense with ferns and podocarps (native 'pine' or conifer trees) such as rimu, kahikatea, matai and miro. Typically this forest is found on the West Coast. The other forest type is beech: dry, austere, spacious, and sparser in the understorey, with a characteristic dappling of light through the canopy. Beech forest is found both sides of the main divide, but is more commonly associated with the east coast. Rainforest seems more Catholic, beech forest more Protestant!

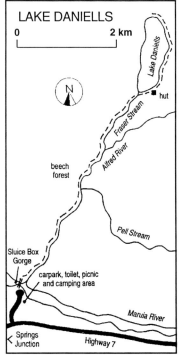

Red beech forest

SONGS OF THE BUSH BIRDS

You are far more likely to hear bush birds than see them, and it takes some skill to identify a particular species. This is partly because most bush birds have a range of different calls: alarm notes, seasonal calls, spring mating calls, day-to-day tunes, differences in male and female songs, and even subtle locality differences within some species. Most bush-bird recordings give you only the basic 'tune'. Timbre or tone is often a key element in identifying a particular species, and with a practised ear it is possible to distinguish the noticeably different timbres of English birds and native species, and with more patience still, pick the timbre of a particular bird species.

Fortunately every bush bird has its niche within the forest, which helps with identification. Robins are curious and territorially aggressive. Fantails and tomtits are usually game to have a look at strangers, partly because we stir up insects. Grey warblers are rarely seen but their long undulating trill is common. Brown creepers are birds of the canopy and flock together. Kakas are generally heard on their own and Lake Daniells is a good place to see them. They habitually favour the mid-height forest slopes and characteristically fly across the valleys at a certain height, usually uttering a creaky-door kraak call. They also have a melodious fluty song. Everyone knows the morepork's peaceful evening call, but in fact it also has a common short screech call that is frequently heard and often puzzles people. Bellbirds and tuis are hard to separate as both have a sweet melodious call, but the alarm call of the bellbird is quite different – a harsh clacking. It often combines the two calls, giving the game away.

There are four recognised beech tree species in New Zealand and one variety, and they have a tendency to hybridise. Red beech is the tallest, with large leaves. Silver beech has a similar fretted leaf to red beech, but is half the size. Hard beech has a leaf closely resembling the red beech but generally larger. Mountain beech and black beech are also difficult to separate, and they both have small oval 'rugby football' type leaves. Actually, some botanists have wondered whether the differences perceived between mountain and black beech are real. Defining what constitutes a species is a notoriously fraught area for the people who make a living out of it – taxonomists (from the Greek *taxis*, meaning order).

From the carpark the track quickly reaches the aptly named Sluice Box Gorge, a deep clear-blue channel where the Maruia River cuts through hard granite.

Then the track sidles through the red beech groves, occasionally crossing matagouri river flats before starting a gentle and subtle climb past the Pell Stream confluence and into the Fraser Stream, which is the outlet from Lake Daniells. The beech becomes silver beech at this higher level and reaches the quiet lapping shores of the lake. A large hut provides a good lunch shelter and there is a short jetty.

TARN WALK & SYLVIA FLATS

Features
Alpine wetland, mosses and lichens, mountain beech forest, orchids, hot springs.

Walking time
Tarn Walk 30 minutes return; Sylvia Flats hot pools 5 minutes.

How to get there
For the Tarn Walk take Highway 7 to Lewis Pass and the St James Walkway carpark. Shelter and toilet.

This is a small gem of a wetland, edged by silver and mountain beech, with limbs made shaggy by hanging lichen. About 20,000 years ago a glacier piled over the Lewis Pass and left behind the debris of poor-draining glacial moraines. The tarn itself was probably formed when a lump of ice melted and left a water-filled depression, usually called a 'kettle lake' or 'kettle hole'. Plants have profusely populated the wetland and, as they grow along the tarn edge, gradually trap soil particles and add to the process of sedimentation that will eventually dry up the tarn.

From the tarn you can see concentric vegetation 'rings' as plant species change according to how dry their root network is. Only such plants as sphagnum moss can live right beside the tarn, then further outwards are the bog turpentine shrubs, then bog pine and red tussocks. One single bog pine can give rise to its own mini-forest, with juvenile shrubs taking root from the parent's own branches and, if the parent dies, leaving a curious ring of outliers intact.

Sundew, an insect-eating plant, likes the open zone between tarn and trees, as does the silvery flax-like astelia. On drier slopes still you find the musk daisy and native harebell. The tree-line, which is mostly mountain beech, is heavily draped with a whitish dangling lichen. This plant thrives in wet, misty conditions and the Lewis Pass area gets more than 3.5m of rain each year.

Along the way there are several plant identification posts, noting both silver and mountain beech, and halfway along the track there's a good view from the lookout up the Cannibal Gorge section of the Maruia River to distant Mount Gloriana (2214m) on the Spenser Range.

43

It is believed that the name Cannibal is a reference to the Maori war parties that used this route for access to the West Coast and its greenstone and would frequently return with human flesh, and even slaves who would later be killed to provide food. Gloriana takes its name from Edmund Spenser's (somewhat dull) poetic epic the *Faerie Queen*. (Lord Burghley summed up this work with a famous riposte when he was asked by Queen Elizabeth I to give a hundred quid to the poet. 'What! All this, for a song?')

The songs are better around the tarn. The grey warbler and bellbird are usually vocal, as well as the chaffinch and the tail-bobbing pipit. Yellow-fronted parakeets are often heard, as well as the mountain parrot (kea) and occasionally its close cousin the kaka.

Dragonflies and damselflies hover about the water's edge, and shy orchids are plentiful in both wet and dry habitats.

Mist over the tarn

Sylvia Flats

There are over 50 hot springs or seepages throughout the South Island, mainly associated with the Southern Alps and the alpine fault. The two commercial hot springs in the South Island are both on the Lewis Pass road: Maruia Springs and Hanmer Springs.

Sylvia Flats is a natural untouched hot spring and is very accessible. The flats are signposted about 8km before Lewis Pass on the Canterbury side. There's a large picnic and carpark area (with toilet), and this small hot spring is just 5 minutes' walk up alongside the Lewis River.

Winter is the best time to visit. The river is lower because the precipitation is locked up in the snowfields and this allows the pool temperature to increase. There are also fewer sandflies (in summer they can be murder). People regularly enlarge the hole and build up the rock wall to keep the Lewis River out.

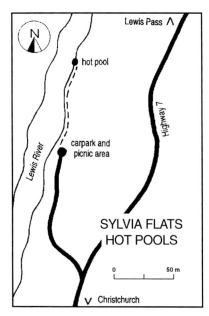

CANTERBURY & BANKS PENINSULA

NIC BISHOP

Ice plant

NAPENAPE

Features

Coastal forest, limestone outcrops.

Walking time

About a one-hour circuit if you take the bush track, but times are really irrelevant. There is a Department of Conservation camping ground for people who fancy an overnight stay, with water and toilets provided. There is a camping charge.

How to get there

From Highway 1 about 110km north of Christchurch (about 3km before the Hurunui River), turn onto Blythe Road and follow the Blythe River past the junction with Stoneyhurst Road (road junctions are well signposted) down to the coast, where a rougher road leads along the shoreline to the large carpark.

This coastal reserve is worth the trouble to get to. A large limestone outcrop runs down to a headland and a steep surging seashore, where swimming is dangerous, of course. But there is plenty to occupy the attention in the shapes and patterns on the limestone boulders scattered on the beach. The limestone cliffs and tors behind the coastal forest look intriguing but there is no practical way to get to them.

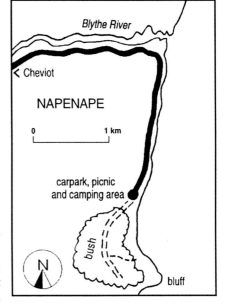

The Amuri limestone at Napenape was formed 60-70 million years ago and is made up of billions of calcite shells from tiny organisms. The result is a platey hard surface.

Though small, this coastal forest is one of the very rare examples of east coast forest still surviving in the South Island. All the plants, such as ngaio and akeake, have adapted to a salt-spray-drenched climate, and have twisted in their attempts to hold on to the dry limestone. Some reach heights of 12m. The forest is dry underneath, with sub-canopy plants such as kawakawa (heart-shaped leaves, often with bits eaten out), karamu, koromiko, and underneath that layer a healthy population of ferns – 19 fern species have been identified so far.

The birdlife is a mixture of typical shore birds, such as red-billed gulls and terns, with introduced finches and thrushes on the farm margins and bellbirds and fantails in the forest itself.

Seals occasionally haul ashore here and, because of the deep waters close offshore, whale sightings are not uncommon. A pod of orca (killer whales) has been spotted barely 500m offshore.

NGAIO

The ngaio is a common tree that is well adapted to the coastal environment, ranging as far south as Otago. In favourable conditions it might reach 10m, but it is usually stunted, having to cope with fierce salt-laden spray and rocky shores. Its glossy leaves are covered with a waxy cuticle that protects them from salt burn. Both the leaves and the fruit are poisonous, and the Maori took advantage of this deadly property by rubbing infusions of ngaio leaves on their skin to repel sandflies and mosquitoes. The inner bark was chewed to relieve toothache, and warmed leaves made a poultice for septic wounds.

SCARBOROUGH HEAD

Features
Sea cliffs and vegetation, spotted shag and seagull colonies, good views.

Walking time
Full circuit from Sumner to Scarborough Head to Taylor's Mistake to the Heritage Trail and back to Sumner takes 3-4 hours.

How to get there
From Christchurch drive 10km to Sumner, and then to the east end of Marine Parade. It's best to park here at the bottom of the hill.

Scarborough Head is a breathtaking place. An old remnant lava tongue has intruded into the sea and been eroded at the base, so that only the harder volcanic rocks remain. The Maori regularly followed a trail over a lowish saddle on the head to avoid the cliffs, until the Europeans rather cheekily busied the cliff-tops with houses and gardens. But it still comes as something of a shock to climb the steps out of the posh suburb and reach the sheer edge of the cliff with its circling, wheeling gulls.

From Marine Parade walk up the Taylor's Mistake road to the first corner in the zigzag (a prominent stone house on the corner) and follow Whitewash Head Road past some smart houses and up a driveway and the signposted track, which climbs a

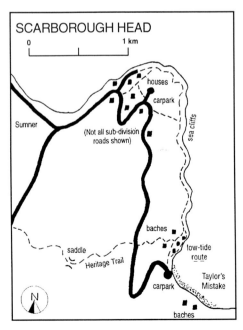

steep set of steps up onto the breezy cliff-top itself. The views are magnificent, especially towards the distant Kaikoura mountains, and seagulls employ the updraughts to spin and rise in an exhilarating ballet.

Grasses occupy the top of the cliff and small lizards dart underfoot. Ice-plants cling to the weathered rock, which drops nearly sheer to the sea. Be careful of the cliff edge; there are no restraining fences at the top.

At the junction, as a shorter exit, you can walk up a grassy track to the road and Nicholson Park, and follow the Scarborough and Flowers tracks back down to Sumner. The main track carries on from the junction to Taylor's

Mistake and can get slippery and muddy after rain as it sidles past gullies and short spurs. The views of the cliffs are dizzying, and you can see the guano-splattered ledges where the spotted shags roost, along with black-backed gulls, red-billed seagulls and pigeons. Birds wheel and spiral between the cliffs constantly, and binoculars will reveal some stunning acrobatics.

At times the track drops quite close to the sea, and there are one or two unofficial side-tracks to the shore itself, but be careful. Close to Taylor's Mistake you can either follow the high-tide-formed track behind the picturesque baches (some of which are isolated at high tide) or, at lower tide, you can walk along the sand at Hobson Bay to the main Taylor's Mistake Beach.

The Maori knew Taylor's Mistake as Te Onepoto, and because of their skills of night fishing the local Maori gained the name Maeaero: 'People of the dark'.

The Heritage Trail starts behind the baches, off the high-tide track. From the Taylor's Mistake surfclub follow the high-tide route back to the signposted turnoff. There is a set of steep steps up to the road, then a poled route is marked across the farmland to the grassy saddle.

The view from the saddle is excellent and you can see both sides of this ancient lava flow that has created a prime piece of real estate for both humans and seabirds. A track goes up from the saddle to the Summit Road, but the Heritage Trail descends a flight of steps to the road at Sumner, and a turn right brings you 1km back to Marine Parade.

NIC BISHOP

Spotted shags

SHAGS AND CORMORANTS

Albatrosses and mollymawks are the same sort of bird, despite the different names, and the same applies to shags and cormorants. There are a dozen species in New Zealand (including the subantarctic islands) and the spotting of a shag squatting on a wharf pile, sunning its outstretched wings, must be one of the commoner seaside sights. Because shags are usually solitary when they are feeding, it is a surprise to realise that they nest in large colonies. At Scarborough cliff the spotted shag colonies are busy with activity. The main breeding takes place in spring with a usual clutch of three eggs, and the young are ready to leave the nest at nine weeks. They practise exercising their wings before making that all-important first launch, tipping into open air some 100m above the surging sea.

BIRDLINGS FLAT & KAITUNA LAGOON

Features
Dryland, wading birds, seabirds, pingao, eels, semi-precious gemstones.

Walking time
A stroll to the red cliff and back to Birdlings Flat would take an hour.

How to get there
For Birdlings Flat take Highway 75 from Christchurch towards Akaroa for 45km, turning at the signposted junction and driving 2km to the large carpark. Do not be tempted to drive further because the gravel is soft. You can also gain access to further down the Kaitorete Spit on Bayleys Road, about 10km. Again watch out for soft sand and gravel close to the shore.

There's a good viewing carpark for the Kaituna Lagoon 1km short of the Birdlings Flat turnoff, and here an old railway embankment gives some walking access further into the lagoon.

Birdlings Flat is a community of baches at the east end of the Kaitorete Spit, the huge tongue of land that separates Lake Ellesmere from the heavy swells of the Pacific Ocean. The landscape has a satisfying bleakness and openness of spirit and is truly a wild place. It takes several visits to appreciate the diversity of wildlife in this area, which many people still dismiss as a wasteland.

Seabirds are plentiful, with black-billed and red-billed gulls and common terns on the shoreline and banded dotterels and skylarks further back in the driftwood and marram grass. There are gannets, the occasional wrybill and spurwing plover on the shore, and Canada geese breed on Lake Forsyth.

One of the most impressive sights is the shags, which nest in colonies on the cliffs of Banks Peninsula, dipping just above the waves as they go off to feed in the morning in large groups and straggle back in less coherent numbers at dusk.

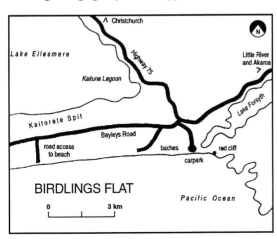

Deep water inshore often creates a spectacular surf, which is dangerous for swimming but popular with surfcasters after kahawai and cod, though dogfish is the most likely catch.

Occasionally seals haul up on the beach, including leopard seals, and Hector's dolphins can be spotted from the shore as well as the occasional whale.

EELS

Eels have had a bad press over the years, with the use of such terms as 'slippery as an eel', but they are remarkable animals with a spectacular life history. Sexually mature eels head out to sea in autumn and travel to a spawning area some 5000km away. They spawn at great depths, perhaps 4000m, and the fertilised eggs hatch into larvae (*leptocephali*) that drift back on currents to New Zealand and change into the transparent 'glass' eel. Then they travel into freshwater streams and make the final transformation into elver – young eels.

Traditionally the Maori have sole eeling rights at Lake Forsyth and just before the autumn migration, when the outlet is closed, long channels are dug into the gravels with a deeper hole at the end. The migrating eels swim into the channels, are spotlit, hauled out with a gaff, and later dried on racks that can be seen behind a few baches. These eels are mostly the short-finned variety, with a smaller proportion of the much heavier long-finned.

Among the gravel, gemstones such as agate, chalcedony and jasper can be found, brought down the Rakaia and Rangitata rivers and dragged up the coast by strong currents.

The Kaituna Lagoon is a 'bay' of the larger Lake Ellesmere, known to the Maori as Waihora: 'water spread out'. Kaituna could be translated as 'eating eels'. Ellesmere's vast flat sheet of water is a breeding wetland and stopover place of international importance for numerous bird species, with some 160 different species being

Leopard seal at Birdlings Flat

Black swans on Lake Ellesmere

recorded. Black swans are notable, as well as many waders, and pukeko on the fringes. In its winter dispersal the white heron (kotuku) can often be seen on the lake fringes, and further inland, especially among cattle, small flocks of white egrets.

Rainfall at Birdlings Flat and on Kaitorete Spit is sparse – 420mm a year – and this creates a 'dryland' of dunes, gravels and grasses. The distinctive orange-red pingao grass can be seen just beyond the baches down the spit. There is a unique flightless moth on the spit, as well as several unusual plants that have adapted to this harsh desert-like environment – notably a prostrate broom. Geckos are seen frequently.

MONTGOMERY PARK

Features
Large totara and matai, native bush, volcanic outcrops, good views.

Walking time
For the bush and big totara tree about 10 minutes return. To reach the highest lookout you should allow 2 hours return. The track is rough in some places.

How to get there
From Christchurch take Highway 75 some 63km towards Akaroa. At Hilltop, the saddle junction, turn left and follow the Summit Road a short way to the signposted park and small carpark area.

Banks Peninsula was once a treasure trove of native bush, almost entirely covered even until European times. The early settlers and timber mills stripped the bush cover, leaving only rare copses of forest, and most of these are poor examples of the glories gone. But Montgomery Park survived, a tiny pocket of excellent bush with big specimens of matai, fuchsia, ribbonwood, lacebark, five finger and the centrepiece, a huge forked totara, 8.5m in girth and 1000-1500 years old. This totara has mates as well, all nurtured on an unusually fertile shelf at an altitude of 400-500m. In addition there have been plantings of native trees not normally found on Banks Peninsula, such as rimu, rangiora and all five species of beech (only two species of beech are native to the peninsula).

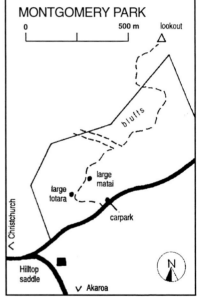

Unfortunately the Big Snow of 1992 devastated parts of Montgomery Reserve, but despite this arboreal carnage the main trees survived and it is interesting to watch the succession that has resulted from these major windfalls.

The track goes in a few minutes to the big totara then wanders past matai trees (some almost 4m in circumference) with their distinctive 'hammer-dent' type of bark, and fuchsia with its peeling orange papery bark. Unusually for native New Zealand trees, fuchsia is deciduous, with distinctive red trumpet-like flowers. Broadleaf are also large trees here, with their obvious shiny lush green leaves, and the understorey has ribbonwood, five-finger, lancewood, lemonwood and mapua. Native bellbirds, yellow-breasted tomtits and grey warblers are all vocal.

TOTARA

Totara live to a ripe old age: many mature trees reach 800 years and exceptional individuals 1800-2000 years – back to the birth of Christ. The several species of totara are widespread throughout the North and South Islands. The wood is red, straight-grained and easy to work, and for the Maori a symbol of strength and goodness. They used it for building canoes (waka) and the carved whare-whakairo. Totara bark was used for thatching. The European found totara useful for more mundane purposes, such as telegraph poles, wharf piles, railway sleepers and fence-posts.

The track sidles off the fertile shelf and under mossy and lichen-covered cliffs, with some open grassy clearings with excellent views over Akaroa Harbour. The track turns steeply uphill over boulders and negotiates a gap in the bluff wall. On the ridge crest the views are excellent, and a short walk up through tussock brings you on top of a rock knob with 360° views to Akaroa Heads, Lake Forsyth and Kaitorete Spit and the characteristic volcanic outcrops that distinguish the skyline of Banks Peninsula.

The Montgomery Track now links up with the much longer Summit Walkway, a track that traces the crest of the peninsula up to the peak of Mount Herbert and on down to Diamond Harbour.

CASTLE HILL

Features
Limestone rocks, karst landscape, tussock grassland, natural stream cave.

Walking time
For Castle Hill rocks allow 2 hours, perhaps more. Cave Stream takes 1 hour.

How to get there
From Christchurch take Highway 73 towards Arthur's Pass some 110km to where a signpost and information board indicate the start of the track. There is a small carpark area. For Cave Stream drive on a further 5km to the signposted picnic area.

Limestone rock formations run down through the east coast of the South Island and outcrop at several places, one of the most distinctive being here at Castle Hill and Cave Stream. The formations are much bigger than you might guess from the road and an exploration will reveal all sorts of intriguing shapes, including archways.

From a geological point of view Castle Hill basin has an isolated and unusual complexity compared with the rocks around it. Whereas the Torlesse Range and Craigieburn Range are mostly greywacke, Castle Hill is a layered mixture of sandstone, siltstone, glacial gravels and even coal measures. The limestone ridges have weathered better than the surrounding rock and so stand out.

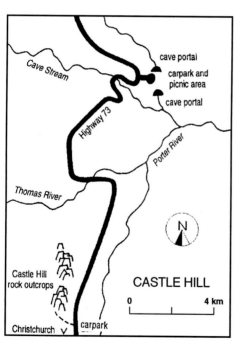

From the small carpark and information board the track skirts under one outcrop of rocks and reaches the main outcrop. Grazing has kept the grass short and there are numerous worn trails that scramble in all directions. With care you can look over a good deal of the formations without getting involved in any of the serious climbs that make this area very popular with rock climbers. Nearly all the rock shapes have an uncanny resemblance to something else: animal-like huddles, or Easter Island statues, or perhaps giant mushrooms.

Both Castle Hill and Cave Stream have been heavily modified by grazing and the ground-hugging hieracium or hawkweed is becoming dominant, but there

Snow on south-facing slopes   *Pause at one of the area's dramatic rocks*

are several rare and unusual plants: cypress whipcord and Brockie's harebell at Cave Stream, and the famous Castle Hill buttercup. Inside the cave lives a rare species of arthropod, a cave harvestman.

KARST LANDSCAPE AND THE CAVE

From Castle Hill it is easy to see the Flock Hill limestone formations, which cover an even wider area. Small canyons, archways and holes are hidden among the jumble of rocks, and often the limestone has been weathered into attractive flutings and scallops. At present you need permission from Flock Hill Station to visit them, but Cave Stream is a public reserve and is an excellent example of karst topography.

The word 'karst' comes from the Yugoslavian and describes what results when limestone is dissolved by weak acids in the groundwater, making unusual pathways into the ground and leaving behind the characteristic sinkhole or 'tomo' (the Maori word for these depressions).

The cave was created when Cave Stream, a tributary of Broken River, diverted itself underground, leaving the dry riverbed. It is a 360m tunnel that twists and turns and can be negotiated by groups led by people who have been through before. It is cold inside, even on the warmest day, and you will get wet, with some deep wades. Torches are essential and on no account should the tunnel be attempted when the creeks are rising. The inlet side of the cave has a small 3m waterfall and you will probably have to have someone belay you up with a rope.

SHARPLIN FALLS

Features
Waterfall, beech forest, honeydew, bush birds, rock lookout.

Walking time
For Sharplin Falls circuit allow 1-2 hours return, for Duke Knob allow 2 hours return.

How to get there
Mount Somers township is 100km from Christchurch. The best road to take is Highway 1 south to Rakaia, then turn onto Thompsons Track. For Sharplin Falls turn right at Mount Somers and follow Highway 72 some 7km to Staveley, then follow the signs 3km to Bowyers Stream carpark, information signs, shelter and toilets.

Tucked in among the foothills, the Sharplin Falls area is a sheltered and charming place with several short walks, lots of bush birds and a pretty waterfall. Those who remember how confusing it was to find the waterfall many years ago will be pleased to find that tracks and signposts have been considerably upgraded and this is now a very suitable place for families and the less fit to visit.

Mount Somers is an old volcanic rhyolite dome, quite distinctive from the greywacke that makes up most of South Canterbury, and Duke Knob is a characteristic outcrop. The forest is a mixture of mountain and black beech with a few scattered southern rata. Rata is sometimes called the Christmas tree because it flowers at that time of year, though the brilliant red that attracts the bellbirds comes not from the petals but from the circle of red stamens. There are also some totara,

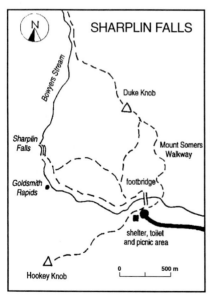

WETA

Weta are nocturnal, flightless grasshoppers which have remained little changed from the age of the dionosaur. There are over 100 species living in almost every environment in New Zealand from the coastline to the alpine slopes. They are broadly divided into five groups: giant weta, tree or bush weta, ground weta, tusked weta and cave weta. The giant weta is possibly the heaviest insect on earth, weighing as much as 70gm, and the cave weta can attain a length of over 30cm from its antenna to its hind legs. However, despite these fearsome statistics and ferocious appearance, wetas are harmless.

NIC BISHOP

Bush weta

matai and kahikatea trees. Typical understorey plants are wineberry (makomako), broadleaf (papaumu), marbleleaf (putaputaweta) and the slender lancewood (horoeka).

There is an attractive short circuit walk (which doubles as a nature trail), as well as other tracks to Duke Knob and Hookey Knob. Across the long swingbridge the well-graded track follows the river and climbs up to a track way. The Sharplin Falls Track drops back down to the river, with a short piece of boulderhopping, and passes a turnoff to the bouldery Goldsmith Rapids.

The track to the waterfall sidles higher and negotiates an elaborate verandah and boardwalk to the gushing 10m falls. On the return you can pick up the high-level track, which climbs and links up with the track to Duke Knob. It's a stiff climb to this lookout, but well worth it for the panoramic view over the dense carpet of beech forest that occupies Bowyers Stream.

WOOLSHED CREEK CANYON

Features
Beech forest, coalmining history, high-country tussock landscapes and views, waterfalls and canyon.

Walking time
4-5 hours return.

How to get there
Mount Somers township is 100km from Christchurch and the best route is on Highway 1 south to Rakaia, where you turn on to Thompsons Track. From the township take the Ashburton Gorge road (to Erewhon) and after about 10km turn off down a signposted and quite rough gravel side-road. It is 3.5km to the Coalminers' Flat picnic area. This is a large grassy sheltered picnic area and campsite, with information boards and toilets provided.

The first part of this walk leads from Coalminers' Flat along the Black Beech Walk for 10 minutes through black and silver beech. The track follows Woolshed Creek then picks up the old jig road to the foot of the jig railway incline. Full four-tonne hoppers of coal would plummet from the mine and a self-acting ropeway would pull up the empty ones. Invariably a hopper would run off the rails from time to time and a mangled example lies at the foot of this incline. The Miners' Track zigzags up the jig incline for a severe 20 minutes' sweat to the bare bleached site of the Blackburn Coalmine.

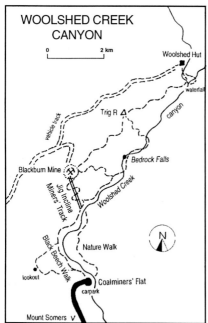

The first coalfield was opened in the Woolshed Creek area in 1864 and eventually a tramway ran from this mine all the way to Mount Somers village, where it joined the newly completed main-trunk railway line in 1887. The tramway up Woolshed Creek itself was built in 1908. The Blackburn Coalmine started life in 1928 but became uneconomic in the Depression and closed down. However it was later worked again in fits and starts until about 1960, but the coal was always poor quality and several underground fires finally closed the mine.

A reconstructed mine entrance has been built, where you can learn about 'Gutsers' and 'Banjos' and marvel at the sheer hard slog of the miners' lives during the Depression years.

A relic of coalmining activities at Woolshed Creek Canyon

From the mine site follow a well-poled track that sidles in tussock gullies along the edge of Woolshed Creek canyon, climbing to Trig R, a splendid viewpoint.

Looking west to the Southern Alps you can see the 3000m Mount Arrowsmith massif and the distant headwaters of the Rangitata River, the mythical land of Samuel Butler's *Erewhon*. (Incidentally, the name is actually an anagram of 'nowhere' rather than the word spelt backwards.)

The poled route nimbly descends past a rocky lookout and drops right down to the gouged and twisted canyon at the head of Woolshed Creek. The track easily fords the dainty upper stream and leads directly to the former musterers' hut. This accommodates eight people comfortably in the trampers' section and there is a sauna hut further upvalley.

The headwaters of Woolshed and Morgan creeks both have an fascinating array of rock outcrops, watercaves, waterfalls and deep crystal pools. A poled track goes from the hut downstream into the Woolshed Creek canyon. The track zigzags neatly under and around bluffs and drops right into the base of the roaring canyon itself, a very worthwhile 10-minute side-trip.

For the return journey back to Coalminers' Flat you can choose a variation by descending a well-marked track off Trig R down to Woolshed Creek and back via Bedrock Falls. This involves crossing Woolshed Creek several times, which is not usually difficult. At the Sidewinder Track junction the silver beech forest is an original pocket of forest that escaped the pre-European fires. Keep an eye out for the unusual strawberry or honeycomb fungi balls that only occur on silver beech.

PEEL FOREST TARN

Features

1000-year-old podocarp forest, alpine tarn and plants, extensive views, bush birds.

Walking time

To alpine tarn and back via Allan's Track and Fern Walk allow 2-3 hours return. Dennistoun bush walk circuit: 1 hour return.

How to get there

It's a 150km drive from Christchurch via Highway 1 south through Ashburton,

branching off at either Ashburton, Hinds or Rangitata. Well signposted.

There is a visitor centre just before the forest, where they also collect payments for campers staying at the nearby campground. The visitor centre is open 9am-5pm summer, winter just weekends, all times subject to change.

The Blandswood road carpark is signposted just past the visitor centre and at the end of its 2km length climbs very steeply (first gear!) on a narrow shingle road for the last few hundred metres.

Mount Peel is the best and virtually last remaining podocarp forest in South Canterbury and has a huge variety of plant species from the forest floor to the alpine tops. There have been 68 species of ferns identified in this tiny 700-hectare remnant forest.

For the tarn and main route to Little Mount Peel take the Deer Spur Track, which quickly passes the two junctions of the Kaikawaka Track circuit. Kaikawaka is the Maori name for the mountain cedar. The Deer Spur Track passes the junction with

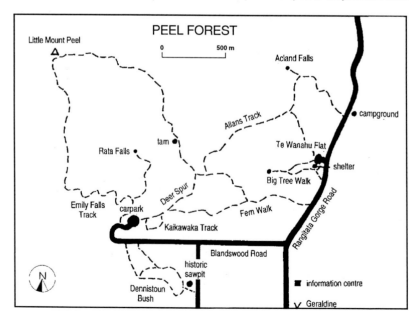

62

the Fern Walk and climbs steadily up through a mixed forest of fuchsia, broadleaf, lemonwood (tarata) and mahoe, with a glossy carpet of ferns.

You will catch occasional views of the plains as the track passes the junction with Allan's Track and enters the upper alpine shrub belt of turpentine, flax and dracophyllums. (Look out for the crimson flowers of southern rata trees at Christmas time.)

The tarn is at an altitude of 900m and might be something of a disappointment if it hasn't rained for a while, leaving little more than a sodden bogland for the frogs to 'rrribit' in (though Peel forest does get an average of about 1100mm of rain a year). There are some splendid specimens of spaniard close to the tarn, with the razor-sharp flowering stalks often reaching over a metre in height.

Walkers on Deer Spur

It is well worth walking up 15 minutes further through the alpine shrubs for the superb views of the Canterbury Plains and the distant Banks Peninsula. On the return you can take Allan's Track as a longer alternative. There's another track junction again

Heart of a spaniard

63

BARBARA BROWN

JEWELLED GECKOS

The jewelled gecko is also present at Mount Peel, varying in colour from an eye-catching bright green to a grey-brown, with whitish stripes or diamond-shaped markings on its back. It's about 150mm long and like most geckos prefers thick cover under logs or rocks, feeding mostly on insects and larvae and usually swallowing the insect whole. Geckos give birth to their young live rather than in the external egg of most other reptiles. They usually undergo a partial hibernation during the cooler months, though a warm day may bring them out to bask in the winter sun. Geckos and skinks are all part of the lizard family, of which nearly 40 species are known in New Zealand, nearly all of them endemic.

almost immediately and you should take the right-hand option, which plunges into a dry fuchsia forest, dropping quite steeply down past a stream to join the Fern Walk. This track ambles along quite close to the forest margin, with many hanging spleenworts (a type of perching fern) dangling off the fuchsia and mahoe. Stop for a breather at Fred's Seat, then on to the Blandswood carpark.

Dennistoun Bush

If you want to see big trees, then take the Dennistoun Bush Walk – it's signposted from the Blandswood road and there's a rest and picnic area here. This short impressive walk leads underneath stately kahikatea, matai and after 15 minutes to a massive 'big mama' of a totara. These trees are all podocarps, native conifers, and come from an ancient family lineage going back a hundred million years. Some of the trees in Dennistoun Bush are up to 1000 years old.

It's worth a side-trip to the historic sawpit, where an information sign shows how the sawmillers did it and a huge stump shows what they did.

ARTHUR'S PASS

Cicada on a flowering manuka

DOBSON NATURE WALK

Features
Alpine tarns, tussocks, alpine flowers.

Walking time
One hour return.

How to get there
From Arthur's Pass village drive 3km to the Temple Basin carpark and the signposted walk.

Arthur's Pass provides a short alpine walk in a splendid setting: a small but perfect tussock bogland at 900m, the tarns reflecting the white massifs of Mount Rolleston and Mount Philistine. The traffic noise might be distracting at first, but soon you will not notice it as you follow the carefully boardwalked track through this delicate environment.

Alpine flowers, despite their sometimes fragile and shy appearance, are undeniably tough. They have to endure extremes of cold and wet, with the occasional baffling period of intense drought. The rainfall on the pass is 5000mm a year, snow can be heavy over winter, and there is little vegetation cover to offer any protection. So the alpine plants have to be cunning, developing small, fleshy or furry leaves to trap moisture and retain heat, and lying virtually dormant throughout the long winter until they burst into flower during spring, which comes later at this altitude in November-December.

Daisies (celmisias), coprosmas, mountain violets, buttercups and hebes are the common flowering plants, usually with yellow or white flowers. This lack of colour variety is often attributed to the lack of specialisation among the insect pollinators, which in New Zealand are usually flies and moths. However, plants such as coprosma add some zestful colours with their variety of coloured berries.

Tussocks are the visually distinctive plants on the walk, mostly red and snow tussock (with their characteristic 'wood-curls' of dead stalks), and the spectacular spaniard with its razor-sharp leaves.

Gentian

Frosted hebe

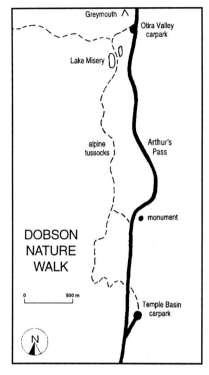

By the tarns and in the boglands you find compact, dense alpine cushions, sundews and snow gentians. The rocks are covered with moss and lichen, and even the tarn waters have their own specialised occupants – diving beetles, damselflies and mayflies. Nature does not waste a good space. Where there is more shelter you find larger shrubs such as dracophyllum, leatherwood and turpentine. The latter has a lovely fragrance and, as suggested by its name, burns well.

There is a good variety of insects, which are a food source for birds such as the pipit, with its characteristic tail flicking. The early settlers and travellers called them snow thrushes, and they are perhaps the most versatile of native birds, for you can find them from the shoreline to the snowline.

Black-backed gulls often make an appearance, incongruously if you associate them only with the seaside, but in fact gulls seem to be great travellers and often have breeding colonies quite deep into the mountains. The most famous mountain bird will not come down if there are any seagulls around, for keas and gulls simply do not get on. But keas do enjoy human company and even if you don't see one you may well hear its haunting call echoing between the mountain faces.

BEALEY SPUR

Features
Alpine wetland, beech forest, braided river, tussocks.

Walking time
To Bealey Hut return about 2-3 hours.

How to get there
From Arthur's Pass village head back towards Christchurch on Highway 73 as far as the bach community at Bealey Spur. Drive up the steep access road to where there is a small carpark and track signpost.

Bealey Spur lifts you out of the valley and offers one of the best views of the intricately braided Waimakariri River. Beech forest at first, with a rare splash of red mistletoe in season, gives way to a heavily scented scrub-line of manuka and then open tussock, with tremendous all-round views. In a nor'wester there is a dramatic contrast between the boiling black clouds on the mountains and the sunny slopes of Bealey.

The track climbs steadily from the carpark, mostly in silver beech and later mountain beech. At the scrub-line the track edges very close to the surprisingly steep and deep gorge of Bruce Stream.

Manuka has been rather a maligned plant in the past, but this scrubby, fast-growing and adaptable tree is mostly beneficial. It invariably provides a good succession base for larger native trees, usually overcoming gorse in the process. As a firewood it is excellent, and manuka honey not only tastes good but also has known medicinal antiseptic qualities.

The track follows poles out of the manuka belt onto an area burnt off for grazing. The views are impressive, and snowberries and daisies hide among the regrown tussocks. Occasionally there is an old gnarled stump, with the odd tangle of fencing wire. The track climbs a tussock knoll that drops through some more beech and follows a boardwalk across a pretty wetland. In winter these tarns freeze over, but in summer they host a wealth of bog plants.

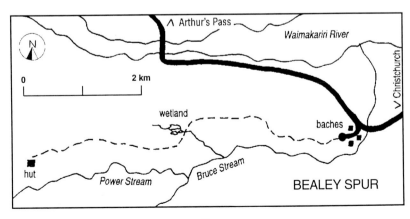

69

The braided Bealey River from Bealey Spur

From the wetland the track climbs open tussocks to the top beech-line again and wanders in among this venerable mountain beech, festooned with the whitish hanging lichen colloquially known as old man's beard, an apt term, although the name sometimes leads to confusion with the introduced noxious weed. One final tussock glade and then Bealey Hut, once known as the Top Hut when Bealey Spur was part of Grassmere Station. The silence is tangible.

MACKENZIE COUNTRY & MOUNT COOK

Dragonfly

OHAU PONDS AND RIVER DELTA

Features

Braided river delta, tussock landscape, black stilts, black-fronted terns, banded dotterels.

Walking time

About 1 hour. There is a good lookout from the dam over the ponds. A number of bird species nest in the riverbed between July and February, and are easily disturbed and often very hard to see. A four-wheel-drive route crosses the riverbed here, and vehicle users should keep a particular lookout for birds. The *Braided River Care Code* pamphlet encourages users not to drive on riverbeds but get out and walk. *Warning:* the ponds area is subject to flooding.

How to get there

On Highway 8, 5km south of Twizel and past the black stilt captive breeding centre, turn down a good sealed road (just over the Ohau River) to Ohau C dam. Plenty of parking and picnic space around the ponds. Just 1km further is the Ohau C camping area, which is right beside Lake Benmore, with good campsites, boat ramps, toilets and effluent disposal for campervans.

Some of the most distinctive habitats in Canterbury are braided rivers. These huge channels of gravel carve right across the Canterbury Plains and the Mackenzie Country, swirling with dust when the nor'wester blows and no doubt cursed by the early road-builders, who had to find a way to bridge these vast multi-channelled streams. Plants and birds have managed to establish themselves quite successfully in these arid and dynamic areas – over 30 bird species have been identified as using the rivers, notably the wrybill and the black stilt.

At the Ohau Ponds (made artificially) visitors get a chance to wander into this extraordinary environment: blisteringly hot in summer, deep frost and sometimes

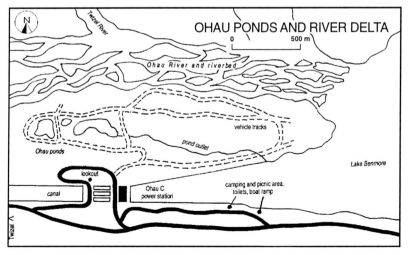

Wrybill

heavy snow in winter. On a fine day the sense of space is marvellous, with the Mackenzie Basin mountains standing out sharply and the inescapable pyramid of Mount Cook in the distance.

Birds often seen around the ponds include paradise ducks, mallard and grey ducks, little shags, spur-winged plovers (with their distinctive yellow eye patch), harrier hawks, song thrushes and grey warblers. Scaup also visit the exit channel of the ponds. On the riverbed in spring you get the arrival of the nesting birds, such as banded dotterels, South Island pied oystercatchers, pied stilts, black-billed gulls and black-fronted terns. They prefer to nest on gravel islands in the riverbed, particularly on the delta draining into Lake Benmore.

Rare visitors include the white heron and New Zealand falcon. Wild black stilts often feed on the riverbed around these ponds.

BLACK STILTS – KAKI

Only about a hundred of these elegant birds still exist (10 years ago there were about 40), and they are found only in New Zealand, living for the most part on the braided riverbeds of Canterbury's Mackenzie Basin. Their population has declined rapidly since the introduction of predators such as cats, stoats and ferrets. Even harrier hawks and black-backed gulls prey on stilts, and habitats have been lost by the choking of the riverbeds by such plants as Russell lupin. Altogether grim times for the black stilt, and breeding numbers have got so low that occasionally they will breed with their cousins the pied stilts.

The Department of Conservation has now established an intensive management of the black stilts, and this programme is part of a larger management scheme to return the Tekapo delta area (the confluence of the Pukaki, Twizel, Tekapo and Ohau rivers) and riverbeds to something like their natural state. This huge project, called Project River Recovery, includes captive breeding of the black stilt and removal of introduced vegetation such as willows and Russell lupins. These taller plants act as cover for predators and can invade the best nesting sites and trap silt, deepening the water channels and causing the loss of shallow-water feeding areas. New wetlands and ponds will be created to balance the loss of habitat from the hydro developments, and to attract the insects on which the birds feed.

The Department of Conservation arranges tours to its viewing-hide 3km south of Twizel, where black stilts are reared in captivity. Bookings are essential – see the Twizel Information Centre.

CLAY CLIFFS – PARITEA

Features
Badland erosion, tussock landscape, braided river.

Walking time
Allow 1-2 hours to explore from the carpark.

How to get there
Access is 3km north of Omarama. Turn on to the Quailburn Road, then the Henburn Road, and drive a few kilometres to a sign. Access is allowed when the sign says 'open', otherwise the farmer's permission is needed. Drive 3km down the farm road to a large sign and park here.

The Mackenzie Country is the wide upland tussock plain between Burke's Pass and Lindis Pass and including Tekapo, Omarama and Twizel. It is a brazen and bleak desert-like landscape, hot in summer, freezing in winter. You do not have to look far to see the cause of these extremes: the Southern Alps, which drain the moist westerly winds by forcing the clouds high over the 10,000-footers that line up along the backbone of this middle region of the mountain chain. The highest spike of all is, of course, the striking Mount Cook or Aorangi.

The Clay Cliffs seem appropriately harsh in this vigorous landscape: a line of eroded pinnacles, a barren and stark imprint of the great erosion processes that have fashioned so much of New Zealand.

From the carpark it is an easy stroll along the vehicle track into the area of the Clay Cliffs where the Ahuriri River cuts in close to the bank. Hieracium often covers the ground where there is no grass. The vehicle track winds up to the base of the steepest pinnacles, and a trail leads through a narrow slot into a crumbling ampitheatre.

CLAY CLIFFS – PARITEA

0   250m

Omarama ∧

carpark

pinnacles

Ahuriri River

four wheel drive road only

N

The local birdlife of yellowhammers, rock pigeons, chaffinches and song thrushes greet newcomers with a boisterous flurry of alarm calls.

The cliffs are big, some 30-50m high in places: spectacular, but take care! Some lone pinnacles are topped with a cap of turf and are certain to crumble soon. There is a real danger of falling debris, so try to avoid becoming a part of the erosion process.

Clay Cliffs is in fact a misnomer for they are layers of gravel and silt, geologically quite young. They were deposited by sheets of gravel and silt flowing out from the great glaciers that existed 2 million years ago. By contrast, the rocks in the nearby mountains are 250 million years old. These strata have been subsequently tilted and later water erosion cut down through the gravel, leaving distinctive pinnacles and deep ravines. Humans sometimes artificially create similar effects, for example in the gold-sluicing claims around Naseby and Bannockburn where high-pressure jets have made a badlands landscape in places.

Paritea means 'white or coloured cliffs' and several ovens on river terraces opposite the cliffs indicate early Maori occupation. Perhaps they used the cliffs for shelter, and refuge from feuding war parties.

Clay cliffs

The best time to visit the cliffs is in the early morning when the low light deepens the shadows in the ravines and brings out the striated sediment colours.

HIERACIUM (AND OTHER BORN SURVIVORS)

There's an old saying that a weed is a plant in the wrong place. Hieracium (or hawkweed) has certainly earned that title. It is a ground-hugging plant that fills up spaces unoccupied by tussock or grass and is unpalatable to stock. It is a vigorous grower and has spread widely in the Mackenzie area, usually in a partnership with the

NIC BISHOP

rabbits, which eat the grass and clear the area free for hieracium to invade. Curiously, hieracium seed has been exported to Germany for use as a plant along the banks of motorways.

The high country is prone to invasion from unwanted plants: briar is another example, along with gorse and lupin (though the latter is palatable to sheep and does provide a splash of colour). Only slowly are management techniques being evolved to try to tackle these competitors in a more effective way than through the use of burn-offs or herbicides. One has to have a grudging respect for such plants as hieracium, which have managed to beat the best efforts of humans to control them.

BLUE LAKES & GLACIER LOOKOUT

Features
Moraine lakes, glacier terminal lake, black ringlet butterfly.

Walking time
30 minutes return to Blue Lakes, 30 minutes return to Glacier Lookout, and 40 minutes return to Terminal Outlet. To do all three walks allow 2 hours return. Only the more sure-footed and keen should scramble about the moraine.

How to get there
From Mount Cook village drive to the Ball Hut Road, then 8km to the signposted picnic area, carpark, shelter and toilet.

There are two short walks exploring facets of this glaciated landscape. Most people are rather disappointed at the 'absence' of the Tasman Glacier. Instead of the expected vision of a crystal-white river with 'icebergs' calving in a deep blue lake, the visitor sees a huge pile of rubble finishing in a grubby lake and a thick dirty river pouring down the valley. What's gone wrong?

Well, the glacier is there all right, and the rubble is only a metre deep in places, on top of 200m of ice. All glaciers are huge grinding mechanisms, carrying large amounts of mountain debris to the plains. Some of this material is held in suspension in the glacier, but because this glacier is downwasting, the debris is much more evident. The terminal lake was only a few sinkholes 20 years ago, and 50 years ago you would have had to walk *up* from the road to get onto the glacier. The lake is likely to go on increasing in size quite rapidly.

At the confluence of the Tasman and Murchison glaciers upvalley quite a large area of glacier has settled and ponds with rushes and grasses have sprung up, in turn attracting Canada geese and other birds to these strange glacial 'pastures'.

The Blue Lakes (sometimes more green than blue as the algae grow) are three small lakes trapped by the moraine. The sediment has settled, giving them their clear distinctive colour. Good for picnics and a cold dip!

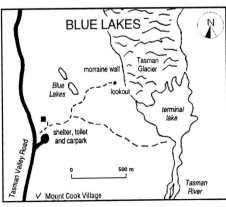

Plants in this environment obviously have to be tough. Around the shelter there is a veritable armada of golden spaniards, a wicked plant of spikes and sharp edges. You will always remember it if you walk into it. Matagouri, a thorny bush that the settlers knew as Wild Irishman also thrives around the lakes. Underneath the larger shrubs grow tussocks, small daisies and cushion plants.

BLACK RINGLET BUTTERFLIES

The black ringlet butterfly has dark brown to satiny black wings with small white dots, and it lays its eggs on the underside of rocks rather than on vegetation, perhaps because the warmth from the rocks speeds up the development of the eggs. It thrives in harsh alpine environments and can survive on the bare glacial moraine of a great glacier such as the Tasman.

It is worth investigating the terminal outlet of the Tasman. The trail crosses grass and matagouri flats and then a stony flood plain to the outlet. Insects can be found even right on the edge of ice and rock, and these in turn attract the pipit, which hopes you might flush the insects out. Most of the birds here are the introduced ones such as the yellowhammer and chaffinch. The grey warbler is a notable native species.

The discoloured grey waters are caused by the sediment or 'flour' held in them, which slowly settles as the river goes downvalley to Lake Pukaki. But enough sediment remains suspended to refract the light in the way that gives both Pukaki and Tekapo their startling and intense aquamarine colour.

Mount Cook buttercups

78

SEALY TARNS & KEA POINT

Features
Mount Cook buttercup or lily, alpine
vegetation, kea, mountain tarns, mountain
views.

How to get there
Drive 2km from Mount Cook village to the
White Horse camping area, shelter and
toilets.

Walking time
1 hour return to Kea Point, 3-4 hours return
to Sealy Tarns.

This is probably the most popular short walk at Mount Cook. The views are
impressive: Mount Cook spiking the air, the thundering ice-cliffs of Mount Sefton,
and the grey moraine walls of the Mueller Glacier and its confusion of lakes and
ponds at the terminal. In November and December Mount Cook buttercups flower
alongside the track, and on most days you will hear (even if you don't see) the
laughing keening kea.

From the White Horse shelter the track winds through groves of alpine toa
toa and matagouri, passes a junction with the Hermitage Track and turns into a
quiet back valley where a profusion of alpine shrubs jostle for space:
dracophyllums such as turpentine scrub, mountain flax, mountain celery, and
hebes, with snowberries, snow totara and daisies underneath. This back valley
is a small, relatively protected pocket and it is striking to compare the plants here

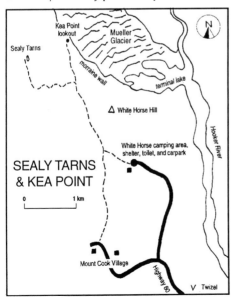

with the more exposed landscape around the Blue Lakes
walk. Bird species are similar in
both areas: grey warblers, chaffinches, yellowhammers etc.

There's a good picnic spot halfway up the Kea Point Track in an
attractive grass glade (take your
own water), but the view from the
final lookout is a little restricted.

The track to Sealy Tarns is very
steep and uncompromising,
rough underfoot and really only
suitable for fitter people. It's a
700m climb and exposed throughout. The tarns are a graceful oasis
in a wilderness of rock and ice,
with alpine flowers fringing the
two ponds.

KEA

A lovable, laughable, crying, clownish, cruel and unforgettable bird, the mountain parrot – sheep killer and tourist tormentor – puts on a show while its mates nip behind and rip the bits off windscreen-wipers and anything else their inquisitive beaks can get around.

Its ke-aa cry is unmistakable, but its distribution and population are matters for conjecture. Most of the nests are in the higher forest and scrub-alpine areas, but it uses the alpine environment for feeding and can come right down to sea level. Most eggs are laid in July-August. The female is the sole incubator; the male never enters the nest.

Keas are mobile, particularly the non-breeders, and males often form small gangs, particularly in tourist hot spots such as the Homer Tunnel or Arthur's Pass, and also on ski-fields, where they can congregate in flocks of 15-20 birds. At this point they become a nuisance.

Keas are a fully protected species, even though individual rogue birds have at times been proven to maim and kill sheep by eating the fatty tissues around the unfortunate beasts' kidneys. Of course it was humans who drove the sheep into these marginal alpine areas in the first place, and then proceeded to kill off keas in quite large numbers because they were a 'threat' to the sheep – a typical human response when we find an animal a tad sharper than we would wish. We can only hope kea numbers will slowly increase and the red flash of its underwing and cackling call will be a popular natural hazard in the future.

NIC BISHOP

WEST COAST

Rata

HEAPHY COAST

Features
Coastline and coastal forest, nikau palms.

Walking time
Scotts Beach circuit is 2 hours return, Nikau Walk 40 minutes return.

How to get there
From Karamea it is a 15km drive to the Kohaihai River and road end. Extensive picnic and camping area, toilets, shelter, phone and lookout track.

This is still an unspoilt coastline. A dark mosaic of hills, often covered with sullen clouds, runs down to the seashore, where abrupt headlands interrupt curvaceous sweeps of yellow sand.

The upper hillsides are covered with beech forest but at the salt-heavy coastline you get a thick profusion of such plants as karaka, kawakawa, tree daisy, kamahi, kiekie and the icon-like nikau palm, which are better adapted. Closer to the sands are the hardier ngaio, coprosma, rangiora, flax, toe toe, lupin and marram grass. Late-evening light can illuminate this landscape the way the sun strikes through the vibrant colours of a stained-glass window.

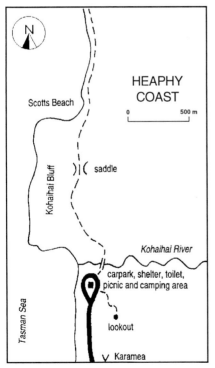

The Nikau Walk is a short nature trail with many plants labelled (including rata), but the more satisfying walk is to Scotts Beach.

Follow the Heaphy Track as it climbs to the Kohaihai Saddle then take the signposted Fisherman's Track, which drops sharply through kamahi and nikau palms to the beach. The left-fork track leads to rocks often favoured by seals – the smell is usually a give-away – while the right track leads to Scotts Beach and a lovely run of sand leading on about a kilometre to the Heaphy Track again. Here you can follow the gentler grade back to Kohaihai Saddle and down to the car-park.

Apart from Scotts Beach it is well worth clambering up the Lookout Track for an overview of the Kohaihai River, and wandering down to the river-mouth itself, where the tea-stained river runs silently into the noisy surf.

Reflections, Kohaihai River

NIKAU PALM

This is a photogenic plant. Close up you can focus on the intricate details of the trunk and fretted leaves; by standing further away (particularly in low light) you can isolate the fern from the rest of the forest, emphasising its undeniable individuality.

Usually about 10m tall, with a tuft of leaves reminiscent of a feather duster, the nikau is the only palm tree found on the New Zealand mainland and a reminder of this country's more tropical neighbours. It is also the southernmost member of the palm family.

The fruits of the nikau are enjoyed by the native birds, particularly the wood-pigeon. Early travellers ate the crisp kernel, which was said to have a sort of nutty flavour. The Maori wrapped food in nikau leaves before cooking it and the large leaves were also used for baskets and thatching.

OPARARA ARCHES

Features
Limestone arches, moa caves, blue ducks, powelliphanta snails.

Walking time
Oparara Arch 30 minutes return; Little Arch 2 hours return; Honeycomb Hill Cave and Top Arch 3 hours return.

How to get there
From Karamea drive north for 10km, then turn inland following the signposts for 11km to the carpark and walking tracks. The road is winding and narrow.

A narrow band of limestone runs along the Oparara valley and the Oparara River has etched a sinuous and sensuous track through this rock, revealing the harder granite underneath and creating three lovely and distinctive arches. Rainforest has disguised this geology and gives Oparara its mysterious and forgotten aura.

The Honeycomb Caves, which contain one of New Zealand's richest fossil collections of many extinct birds, were only systematically explored in the 1980s, and this last resting ground holds the remains of nine different moa species, a giant flightless goose, a flightless wren, and takahe and kakapo. It's as if an earlier, entirely different dawn chorus has vanished.

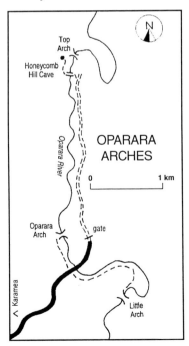

The arches are what people usually come for, and they are impressive. You can walk through the largest, Oparara, which is 43 metres high and 219 metres long. The inside is dry and roomy with stalactites and stalagmites. The Little Arch (Elven Door) is smaller, at 19 metres high and 43 metres wide, and the track actually crosses its roof. There is also a dry cave underneath with stalactites. The smallest and prettiest arch is the Top Arch (Moria Gate), close to Honeycomb Hill. Blue ducks are often present here. Galadriel's Mirror, a rimu-fringed pond, is a signposted walk taking about 30 minutes return.

The strange names were introduced by the Friends of the Earth from Tolkien's book *Lord of the Rings*. It seems ironic that a conservation group that tries to restrict the range of imported plant and animal species has quite happily introduced a clutter of exotic names.

Once you've seen the arches, don't forget the podocarp beech forest that sets the scene, with rimu, matai and kahikatea overtopping the red beech, and a thick understorey of shrubs such as quintinia, mahoe and putaputaweta. There are also two short caves to explore, both five minutes walk in. Crazy Paving has a distinctive mud floor, and Box Canyon is a high cavern. Take a torch.

Oparara is home to quite large bird populations, including blue ducks, great spotted kiwis, kakas, keas, tomtits, bellbirds, parakeets, wood pigeons and tuis. On the ground look for the large-shelled powelliphanta snail, a nocturnal carnivore that feeds on worms. The shells are colourful spirals of brown, gold and orange, and it is illegal to remove them, even when empty. Rats, wekas and even keas and kakas prey on these lsnails, the largest of which may be 10-20 years old.

Access to Honeycomb Hill caves is by guided tour only, arranged through the local information centre. Apart from the fossil remains there are many interesting speleotherm formations in this 18,000-year-old cave complex, riddled with over 30 entrances and containing one of New Zealand's largest native spiders, *Gradungula*, with a leg span of up to 12cm.

Powelliphanta snail

BLUE DUCKS – WHIO

Blue duck

The Maori name 'whio' is aptly derived from the male bird's distinctive whistle, to which the female usually replies with her equally distinctive grunt. Blue ducks are river specialists that dislike flying. They live mostly in fast-flowing waters and try to avoid predator disturbances by using the currents and pools of the river – swimming seems too inelegant a term for this sharp and graceful evasion practice. They live on insect larvae and forage among the stones. Whio are usually seen in pairs, which establish clear territories about a kilometre long, and a river such as the Oparara will hold several pairs. It's believed that they only reluctantly fly between catchments and so are slow to establish themselves elsewhere once driven out of an area. Habitat changes, as well as introduced predators, have seen blue ducks decline in number, although their love of wilderness regions with fast-flowing rivers hardly encourages frequent sightings. They nest in July-August and the chicks are independent after six months. An established pair can expect to live for about seven years.

CHARMING CREEK

Features
Granite gorge, waterfall, tramway, mining history, glow-worms.

Walking time
Right through is 3-4 hours (you will need transport at the other end).

To Mangatini Falls through the gorge is about 2-3 hours return.

How to get there
From Westport drive 35km to Ngakawau. The walkway is signposted just before the river, and it is 200m to the carpark.

It is no accident that you can smell coal smoke as you drive into Westport. King Coal has been one of the economic mainstays of this area for many years and is likely to remain so. The Charming Creek Walkway takes advantage of an old coal railway to explore the stunning landscape from which the miners had to wrench the black gold. The walkway is well signposted, with informative signboards detailing the coal-extracting operation. From 'The Bins' terminus you quickly follow the slick dark waters of the Ngakawau River through the S-bend of Irishmen's Tunnel (a mistake in alignment) and through another 'tunnel' that is in fact a natural rock arch. The granite gorge is at its narrowest here as the tramway crosses the long suspension bridge with excellent views of the Mangatini Falls. Just before the bridge a side-track goes down to the foot of the falls close to the spray curtain.

There's another 50m tunnel, a boardwalk verandah, and then the confluence of Charming Creek and Ngakawau River. Fit and keen people can scramble down to the confluence rocks and watch the black Ngakawau River emerge from its secretive top gorge. The river always carries a thin line of foam and creates elaborate swirls and patterns as it joins the Charming.

From here the walkway changes character, leaving the gorge and entering a cut-over landscape of mine debris, relics of the old steam sawmill, a sulphur hole and the Papa Tunnel.

At the warmer coastal end of the walkway typical plants are the karamu, kiekie and kawakawa, with nikau palms and northern rata on the hillslopes overlooking

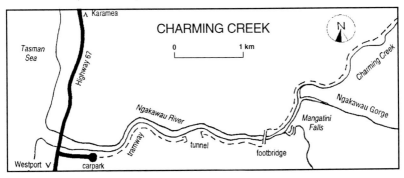

FERNBIRD – MATATA

This is a rarely seen but not uncommon bird that likes the scrubbier forest fringes and does well in pakihi and cut-over areas – one of the few native birds to accustom itself to human encroachment. You can often attract fernbirds by imitating their call and

making a clicking sound with two stones, and you can usually hear them in the cut-over section of the Charming Creek. They are weak fliers, preferring to move stealthily through the dense ground cover. About the size of a thrush, their whitish bodies are streaked black and brown and they have a long straggling tail.

NIC BISHOP

the gorge. In the cramped and often gloomy spaces of the gorge itself you find silver beech and the unique *Celmisia morganii* daisy, found only in the Ngakawau Gorge. Out of the gorge the rimu forest that once would have dominated has gone and regenerating manuka has grown up, with rimu regenerating underneath. You will find silver pine and mountain toatoa in wetter areas.

GLOW-WORMS

There are glow-worms in the tunnels and by the wet dark banks of the railway cuttings. Pretty things, but on closer acquaintance they seem rather more sinister. Glow-worms are the carnivorous larvae of a gnat, transparent, living in a small tube from which are hung sticky, silky threads or feeding lines that trap their prey – mainly midges. The midges are attracted to the luminescence, which has been calculated at one nanowatt (one thousandth of a millionth of a watt). The cause of the glow is the oxidisation of a chemical called luciferin, which is present in the glow-worm. The male shines with a blue-green light but the female is reddish, and the hungrier they are the more they glow! Before emerging as a flying gnat, the female larva pulls in the loose threads (to avoid trapping herself when she exits) and, suspended from a single thread, emits a strong pulsing light to attract the males. She is immediately mated on exit and has a one- to three-day existence to lay her eggs to continue the cycle. The males may mate again, and may themselves get entangled in the threads and provide a meal for other larvae.

CAPE FOULWIND

Features
Seal colony, wekas, pukekos, coastal views.

Walking time
30 minutes return to the seal colony, 2-3 hours one way for the entire walkway.

How to get there
From Westport it's 12km down the Carters Beach road to the large carpark and toilets at Tauranga Bay.

This is one of the best and most popular short walks on the coast and in the breeding season the New Zealand fur seal colony is spectacular, with as many as 150 pups in about March. A friendly colony of wekas haunts the carpark at Tauranga Bay, which is a fine sandy sweep of beach, and it takes some imagination to picture horse coaches steaming along this stretch in the goldrush of the 1860s.

Abel Tasman named this point Clyppygen Hoeck or 'rocky corner' and it is likely that this, rather than Okarito, was his first landfall of New Zealand in 1642. Dumont d'Urville in 1827 called it Les Trois Clochers or 'the three steeples', but Captain Cook had named it Foulwind in 1770 and it still seems appropriate today as the squally seas are frequently stormy.

From Tauranga Bay a well-maintained track climbs up onto the headland and leads down to the lookouts over the seal colony. The fur seal is found only in New Zealand waters and off the south coast of Australia.

Seal colony

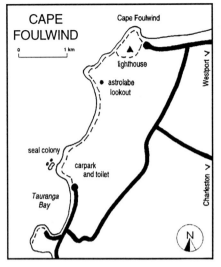

CAPE FOULWIND

Cape Foulwind

lighthouse

astrolabe lookout

seal colony

carpark and toilet

Tauranga Bay

Westport

Charleston

The seals arrive to give birth in November and December and by March the numbers of pups are at their peak, and a lively lot they are. They get together in groups to play games that look for all the world like king of the castle and tag. Female seals are sexually mature at three to four years and males at six to seven, though the latter rarely become active until nine or ten years old, when they are strong enough to compete against other bulls.

Females and pups stay close to the breeding place most of the year while solo males move away, hauling ashore all around New Zealand's coastline. Seals can travel for hundreds of kilometres but their migration habits are still not widely understood. The principal diet of fur seals consists of squid, octopus, lantern fish and barracuda, with most feeding done at night. Colonies usually have a pungent smell, a useful early warning signal for unwary humans.

From here the track becomes a lot muddier and can be further churned up by cattle. After a short sidle and climb you reach a plaque and a perspex-enclosed astrolabe, which was of the type Abel Tasman used when he first arrived in New Zealand. The track then sidles around more farmland to the lighthouse. Here it's a good idea to go down to the shore and follow the banking of the old railway line, which was used for moving quarried rock. On stormy days this is a wild piece of shore. Watch out for seals here – stragglers can often be spotted snoozing on the rocks.

WEKAS

The European pioneers knew this inquisitive and flightless rail as a woodhen, praising it for its eating qualities and condemning it for its thieving. An aggressive, curious nature has enabled the weka to cope with humans and their introduced predators, indeed to thrive in almost semi-urban areas. There are several sub-species of weka; the Chatham Island version, originally imported from the South Island, is so common it is considered a pest.

Wekas eat anything: berries, insects, lizards, mice, rats, young rabbits, shellfish, grasses, seeds, vegetable crops, snails and the eggs and young of other birds. They even eat their own dead! Since it is unlikely you will see a kiwi (except in an aviary) enjoy the weka – it's a tough, adaptable and cheeky bird.

PUNAKAIKI BLOWHOLES & TRUMAN TRACK

Features
Pancake rocks and blowholes, coastal vegetation, tidal platforms, sea-caves.

Walking time
Pancake Rocks 30 minutes circuit, Truman Track 30 minutes return.

How to get there
Drive to Punakaiki on Highway 6 (60km from Westport, 45km from Greymouth) to the information centre, cafe, tearooms, toilets, shop and large carpark. The Truman Track is 2km north.

These two stunning short walks, though not connected, illustrate the fearsome and magical aspects of the Paparoa coastline. The mountains come right down to the spray-drenched shoreline and the encounter causes dramatic headlands, sea-stacks and etched tidal platforms.

It's a rich wildlife area. Seals come ashore up and down the coast and there are many shag colonies. Little blue penguins nest in various places along the coast (note the penguin signs on the highway) and occasionally Fiordland crested penguins make visits. Gulls are common, and the black-backed gull nests in spectacular colonies high above the bush-line, several thousand feet up on the Paparoa Range. Oystercatchers, banded dotterels, terns and pipits are common on the seashore, and the Westland black petrel breeds just south of Punakaiki in a bush colony.

Punakaiki is a justly famous tourist honey-pot. A well-graded track (suitable in places for wheelchairs) leads through a dark coastal forest of nikau, mahoe, rata vines, kiekie, tree ferns and cabbage trees, followed by a fringe of flax and then out onto a rugged headland. The reason for

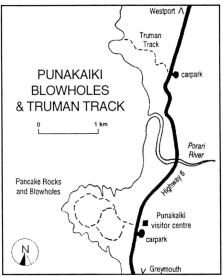

the pancake name becomes obvious straight away: the limestone rocks are layered in elegant patterns like a stack of thin pancakes, forming huge columns.

The rocks were formed by sedimentation of shell debris, accumulated and compressed over millions of years and then uplifted. The sea then forced its way under this geological formation, creating surge chambers and blowholes that can explode with extra-ordinary power in the right weather conditions. Please keep to the marked tracks: the dangers are obvious.

FLAX – HARAKEKE

Flax is a distinctive coastal plant that prefers wettish ground but will grow just about anywhere and its familiar 3m stiff red-petalled stalks have become a common sight in suburban gardens. Nectar feeders such as  tui, bellbirds and silvereyes love the sweet juice and act as pollinators for the plant.

There are two species of native flax and many varieties. Some types were used for rope-making by early Europeans, but the uses to which the Maori put this plant were wide-ranging and ingenious. They made rope, of course, and used thinner fibres as a sort of string. Flax sandals called parara were made for travelling, and kawa was the name given to the flax pack-straps. Dry flax stalks were bundled together to make rafts or mokihi, and the broad leaves were entwined to make a base for making bread. The leaves also had food cooked in them.

Even on a calm day Punakaiki will not disappoint, as the track cautiously circumnavigates a surging sea chamber and investigates the many different geological structures and quirks. Mat plants and some shrubs such as koromiko cling to the edges of the blowholes, which have appropriate names such as Sudden Sound, Chimney Pot and Putai (seaspray). On a clear day you can see Mount Cook in the distance.

The Truman Track is another easy, short and satisfying walk. First you pass through the coastal 'jungle' that the Maori had to negotiate in their regular journeys up and down the coast, with the characteristic weeping rimu, matai, tangles of white-limbed kiekie and the dark twisting supplejack, then through flax and tough mats of coastal herbs before the upper sea-rock platform. Take care here: the rocks are notoriously greasy. The colours of seaweed, lichen and algae are in striking contrast to the dark glistening rock.

A ladder goes down onto a semi-circular beach where shallow sea-caves have been carved out, and at low tide you can easily get round the sculpted rocks to the next bay and fossick among the tidal platforms.

BLACK PETREL COLONY GUIDED TOUR

Operating from close to Punakaiki, this tour takes visitors to a Westland black petrel colony, the only one of its kind on the mainland, and to the nesting sites in the bush, where the birds make their dramatic twilight return. See the information office at Punakaiki.

KAHIKATEA FOREST WALK

Features
Kahikatea trees, mosses and lichens, bush birds.

Walking time
20 minutes circuit.

How to get there
From Hokitika follow the signs to Kaniere and then on to Lake Kaniere, about 17km. At the Sunny Bight foreshore picnic area there are carparks, toilets and signposted walks.

This is a short stroll in an unexpectedly impressive patch of kahikatea forest. A dense swathe of ferns on the ground, then mosses and lichens on the trunks of trees, and epiphytes (perching plants) high up – greenery from the ground to the sky. Kahikatea or white pine is New Zealand's tallest native tree, with some specimens reaching 60m. Because they like the fertile floodplain soil they were among the first to be cleared when humans needed space for agriculture. The trunks were

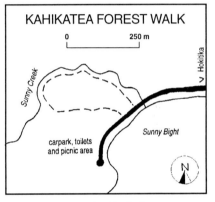

straight and useful for construction, and because the wood had little 'flavour' to it, it was used extensively for butter boxes in New Zealand's early exporting days.

Kahikatea is astonishingly productive in terms of fruit, and needless to say this attracts wood pigeons, bellbirds and tuis, which in turn help to disperse the kahikatea's seeds. Other prominently vocal birds are the fantail (piwakawaka), grey warbler (riroriro) and its parasite the shining cuckoo, a summer visitor.

Kahikatea fruit and seed

The understorey is rich, including kaikomako, mahoe, tree fern, coprosma and many ground ferns – there are over 50 species of fern in the Lake Kaniere Scenic Reserve. Epiphytes are equally diverse: liverworts, mosses, orchids and ferns. Plants such as kamahi often begin life as perching seedlings on tree ferns and so avoid the gloomy low-life chances of the forest floor, which gets only 1 per cent of daylight. Vines such as supplejack (black), rata (red) and bush lawyer (prickly) survive by climbing quickly towards the light using any convenient tree trunk. Bush lawyer is a close relative of the raspberry and produces very similar raspberry-like fruit.

SETTLING DOWN

When the first European adventurers and settlers arrived in New Zealand they were faced with a considerable naming problem: whole forests of unfamiliar plants, strange birds, weird insects. The Maori names were often incomprehensible to the early settlers so they took the lazy way out and introduced a whole species of sometimes inventive, sometimes daft, substitutes.

Look at the podocarps, for instance. Kahikatea was 'white pine', rimu 'red pine', matai 'black pine', miro 'brown pine'. Easy, eh? The beech forest was often called birch and was still labelled thus on many topographical maps of the 1940s.

The white alpine berries of *Gaultheria antipoda* were a cinch for the name 'snowberries'; 'bush lawyer' scathingly refers to the clinging, prickly vine; and the tasty leaves of horopito were quickly dubbed 'pepper tree'. It was also known as 'bushman's painkiller' because chewing the leaves supposedly eased toothache. Captain Cook tried manuka leaves as a substitute for tea, so 'tea tree' it became.

Some of the birds received more imaginative names. 'Snow thrush' for the pipit is charming, as is 'parson-bird' for the tui, in reference to the distinctive white ruff on the bird's throat. Weka became 'woodhen' because it looked a bit chicken-like and lived in forests, but why did bellbirds became 'mockies'? The shining cuckoo was called 'whistler', and the long-tailed cuckoo was nicknamed 'screecher' or 'screamer' after its long drawn-out wail. Actually the Maori name 'koekoea' also seems to imitate the call.

The 'morepork' was surely the silliest name dreamed up. The soft night call of this owl doesn't actually sound very much like the words 'more pork' – unless you're hungry, and perhaps the early settlers often were.

NIC BISHOP

Morepork

94

WANGANUI HEADLAND

Features
Coastal headland and lookout, shearwater colony, pakihi wetland, historic pack track.

Walking time
Full circuit about 2-3 hours.

How to get there
From Harihari on Highway 6 turn off down Wanganui Flat Road (the walkway is signposted) and drive towards the coast some 20km to the small carpark.

Mount One One is a curious and distinctive morainic outcrop at the mouth of the Wanganui River. 'It had the honour of being the first scene in Westland that appeared in the *Illustrated London News* ... Home people must have had some fun over the name, so suggestive of the first numeral, and wondered at Colonial nomenclature, never dreaming the name One One is Maori,' wrote explorer Charlie Douglas. The meaning of the name is still obscure: 'oue' is an alternative that has been suggested. But there's no doubt it is a superb lookout over the coastline and Wanganui river mouth.

From the carpark the coastal walkway passes several idiosyncratic white-baiters' baches and crosses a deep black swamp creek before cutting across a scrubby terrace to the base of Mount One One. Steps lead up to the excellent viewing platform and you might notice on the way up the numerous burrows

Beach and Mount One One

Staircase to lookout

95

underneath the stairway, home to a sooty shearwater colony. It was something of a mistake putting the walkway right over the colony and it has driven away some of the nesting birds.

From One One drop back to the track junction and stroll along this driftwood-strewn beach. At low tide it is quite easy to get around the point, scrambling over some large rocks, but there is a high-tide alternative signposted.

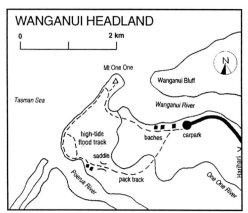

WANGANUI HEADLAND

The Poerua River is not as large as the Wanganui and in winter river levels can get so low that the sea builds up a permanent gravel bar across the mouth. The track skirts the river and reaches some more whitebaiters' shanties before turning inland and following the well-laid line of the old pack track as it crosses a low 100m saddle and drops down to the pakihi swamp on the other side, and the carpark.

SOUTH WESTLAND

Kamahi seedling perched on a tree fern

OKARITO LAGOON

Features
Estuary and lagoons, white herons, coastal forest, mountain lookout.

Walking time
Okarito Trig 1 hour return, Three Mile pack track to lagoon (with low-tide beach option) 3-4 hours return.

How to get there
From 'The Forks' turn off 16km south of Whataroa on Highway 6 and travel along the sealed road 13km to Okarito. Camping ground, information (in the wharf shed), signposted walks and boat launching ramp. Tide tables at the beach noticeboard.

Okarito went from nowhere to nowhere. After the discovery of gold, particularly the rich beach sands of the Three Mile and Five Mile, Okarito grew fast until by December 1865 it had a population of 800, with 33 stores. 'Everybody who does not dig sells grog, and everybody who digs drinks copiously,' an early newspaper account recorded, which made for a 'remarkably rowdy class of inhabitants and visitors'. All too soon the rich beach sands were exhausted and Okarito's glory years were two, perhaps three in number. Charlie Douglas saw the final decline of Okarito town. 'It made a desperate effort to reach the borough stage but ignominiously failed. A town council was selected who at once started to tax the citizens, but as they had no power to do so, no one was fool enough to pay, so as there were no funds even for the councillors' beer, it was judged best to retire.'

There is still a small settlement at Okarito, with an incongruous pillar commemorating Abel Tasman's first sighting of New Zealand – although it is now believed he first saw land much further north at Cape Foulwind.

But the lagoon itself is magic. You can hire canoes and quickly paddle into a rich birdlife with shags doing sentry duty on old rotting piles, black swans clustering, and the deliberate, white stalking figure of the kotuku as it goes about its solitary hunting activity. At the Okarito river delta you can paddle up deep canals of rainforest lined with flax, with paradise shelducks and bellbirds making a kerfuffle as you glide along. Get advice on the tides – it's best to catch a high tide going in and it's easy to get stranded on mudflats – but there are marvellous rewards in seeing the great peaks of Cook and Tasman, the latter looking like the outstretched wings of a gull.

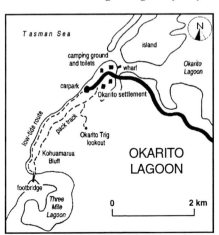

Okarito Trig is an impressive short walk, best on a sunny day. The pack track to the Three Mile is in excellent condition and comes out by a bridge that crosses the swamp outlet of the Three Mile lagoon. With a low tide you can follow the beach back to Okarito, rock-hopping and keeping an eye out for the occasional seal.

WHITE HERONS – KOTUKU

Maori legend has it that the white heron is so rare it is seen only once in a lifetime. In fact they are more 'spottable' than you might think, as their winter dispersal takes them to estuaries all over New Zealand. They breed only at Waitangiroto, a river just north of Okarito lagoon, and the nests are perched high up in the kahikateas as the birds jostle and squabble about the colony. There are often royal spoonbills and little shags nesting in association with the white herons. Gerhard Mueller saw the colony in 1865 and left a lovely and accurate description. 'But the crowning beauty was a cranery which I discovered up the river, and that was a glorious sight... Of these birds (near 4ft high) imagine seeing around you 50 to 60, sitting on high pines and lower trees, in a circle of about 150 yards, their pure white feathers shining in the sun. It was a glorious sight – I gave up pulling and watched the tribe for a long time. They were not at all shy – kept up a continual "plappering" among themselves, and seemed to be astonished at me more than afraid.'

The only public access to the white heron colony at Okarito is a guided tour from Whataroa, which includes a jetboat ride downriver and a short guided walk to the hide. See information centres at Whataroa or Franz Josef.

White herons on Okarito Lagoon, with Mounts Tasman and Cook behind.

FRANZ JOSEF GLACIER

Features
Glacier, waterfalls, schist rock.

Walking time
To the glacier terminal lookout and back 2 hours.

How to get there
From Franz Josef village on Highway 6 it is 5km to the glacier carpark, shelter, information signs and toilets. The narrow road can get busy.

Most of the glaciers in New Zealand are well beyond reach. You might spot them glinting in the distance, or pass over them at 30,000 feet while having your plastic lunch and not even realise what those white squidgy things are. But uniquely on the West Coast there are two glaciers you can almost touch – the Fox and the Franz Josef. Both are superb, but the Franz Josef is the more scenic.

Some books refer to glaciers as frozen rivers of ice, and although this description is okay as a brief summation, it belies a glacier's complexity. It takes immense forces to bring a glacier about. High precipitation in the headwaters, falling usually as snow, is the first trigger. Rainfall on the West Coast is about 3m but on the Franz Josef névé it is an incredible 15m a year. Intensely cold temperatures are needed to prevent the snow from melting; pressure, usually of the snow's own weight, to compact the snow into a dense mass; and gravity to pull the mass downwards.

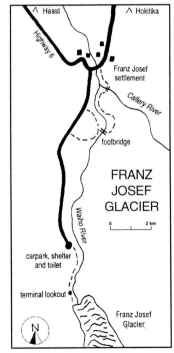

Some 1400 years ago Franz Josef was part of a large ice sheet but over the last 300 years it has retreated dramatically. Then in 1994-95 it began an even more dramatic advance towards the coast, drawing thousands of visitors to view the glacier from a safe point well away from its terminal, from which huge blocks of ice would occasionally fall. The short-term outlook for this particular glacier is a steady increase for the late 1990s. But overall, glaciers around the world are slowly retrenching.

One of the most impressive things about Franz Josef is not the glacier but the rock walls that have been exposed as the glacier has retreated. The main rock type of the Southern Alps is greywacke, a crumbly 'weetbix' rock, which is carried down by the glacier as moraine. But the Franz carves its way through a layer of much harder metamorphic schist rock, which

Glacier walk

has been contorted into incredible wave-like shapes and is strikingly evident as you walk up to the glacier. The sheer rock faces are a great playground for waterfalls, especially after a West Coast downpour, and for the hardier types a trip to the glacier in stormy conditions is exhilarating.

The climate can be vigorous in this cold deep valley, so take some warmish clothing and some nibbles. The trail is well marked but it is not recommended you go onto the moraine of the glacier itself except as part of a guided group.

GLACIER JARGON

There's a language of glaciers. The névé is the top part of the glacier, the huge collecting snowfield. New snow compresses the air out of old snow to form firn, which in turn is compressed into blue ice. Gravity shifts the mass downward, and under the strain crevasses appear, which are the distinctive linear cracks that cross the glacier, especially where the incline increases or there's a corner. Where the glacier is squeezed at the narrowest and steepest part of its descent you will see the ice-fall, a mangled bunch-up of crevasses and seracs, isolated pinnacles of ice. Rock that has been crushed and dragged down by the glacier is called moraine. It collects at the sides of the glacier, on the surface and at the terminal. Often glaciers have terminal lakes, though this is not the case with the Fox and Franz, where you can the see the river gushing out from an ice-cave directly under the glacier. The 'milkiness' of the river is caused by glacial flour, which is a fine mass of silt and grit eroded by the glacier and suspended in the water.

LAKE MATHESON

Features
Lake and reflections, rainforest, bush birds.

Walking time
1-2 hours circuit.

How to get there
From Fox Glacier village drive 5km to the signposted carpark. Toilets beside the cafe.

Lake Matheson is one of the most famous of New Zealand's tourist traps – it is both corny and fantastic at the same time. The reflections can be so good that they are disorientating, and are best in the morning and evening when the wind is silent and the light is soft. The carefully constructed boardwalk around the lake seems way over the top and the Reflection Island platform is like a bit of Disney – but it still works, it's still magic. Bird sounds float over the lake, Nikons click and buzz ...

Lake Matheson was formed from a large chunk of ice that got left behind when the Fox Glacier ice sheet retreated about 14,000 years ago, leaving mounds of moraine debris that trapped the resultant lake – what is technically called a kettle lake. Forest grew around the lake and its famous reflections partly result from the brown colouration of the water, caused by organic matter leached from the humus on the forest floor.

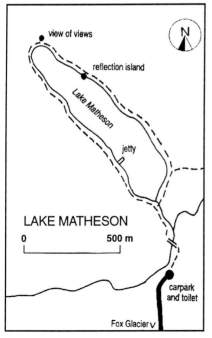

The track crosses the Clearwater Stream bridge and follows the tiny and densely overlayered outlet stream to the lake and the first viewpoint. You need to go to the head of the lake and climb up to the View of Views platform to get the classic tablemat and calendar view.

A few minutes on there's Reflection Island, then the track keeps to forest around to the farmland. On frosty misty mornings these paddocks with their gnarled and isolated kahikatea trees can sometimes provide better photos than the better-known set pieces. The rainforest consists of tall podocarps such as kahikatea, rimu and matai, along with a lush under-storey of shrubs and ferns. Look out for perching orchids on logs and stumps. The calm surface of the lake accentuates any bird sound and the

Paradise duck

bush birds you are most likely to hear are the bellbird, yellow-breasted tomtit and fantail, as well as the irritatingly cheerful song thrushes and the alarm squawks of blackbirds. On the water paradise ducks honk in lugubrious pairs and mallards fossick in the reedy edges.

THE SOUTHERN ALPS

How come a continent the size of Australia has no decent mountains to speak of while little New Zealand is jam-packed? Well, Australian rocks are much older and have been worn away by millions of years of erosion. New Zealand, however, has young mountains, forced upwards by the action of the two continental plates it straddles. This remorseless tearing of the geological fabric gives New Zealand its earthquakes, its hot pools, its volcanoes and its young unstable mountains – note the huge chunk that peeled off Mount Cook in 1991 (fortunately without affecting the Lake Matheson reflection!). The alpine fault (a giant stretch mark) is just a few kilometres away from Lake Matheson, following the main highway, so the appearance of serenity and permanence that visitors feel when they visit the lake is somewhat illusory. The landscape is constantly changing.

GILLESPIES BEACH

Features

Coastal forest, lagoon, seal colony, historic tunnel, lookouts.

Walking time

To the lagoon and back 2 hours, to the historic tunnel and lookout 3 hours return, to the seal colony 4 hours return.

How to get there

From Fox Glacier (Highway 6) it's 20km to Gillespies Beach, and 11km of this is unsealed. This is a narrow road with many blind corners. Carpark, toilets and signposted walks.

A wild coast with a battering surf and driftwood piled high on the beach – Gillespies has presence. On a fine day the mountains stand above the black swamp lagoon like a mirage and the spume from the surf creates its own mist. Sunsets are very fine.

Gillespies got its name from James Edwin Gillespie, who detected payable gold on the beach sands here in 1865. A small town sprang up but it did not last long. The explorer Charlie Douglas commented in the 1890s: 'Gillespies got beyond the calico era and almost attained the dignity of weatherboard, but not quite. It now contains a few diggers' huts, a store and school house, with of course the usual pub, but its life cannot last that long as the beach is nearly worked out. It has however lasted longer than any of the diggers' townships of Southern Westland and contains a chapel – still standing – a building none of the others ever possessed.'

Gold dredges later turned over much of the beach frontage, but apart from a few remnants of metal there's hardly a thing left to mark the glory days – just the cemetery and the proliferation of gorse.

There are a lots of walks to choose from at Gillespies. The dredge ruins are slowly slipping into the mire and require more imagination each year, so the pictures on the signs are helpful. More worthwhile is the walk north to the lagoon, with its trestle bridge and the dark tidal water offering some dramatic reflections.

GILLESPIES BEACH

0   2 km

seal colony

tunnel

trig lookout

footbridge

N

Gillespies Beach

lagoon

Otorokua Point

Whelan Creek

carpark

Fox Glacier

Across the bridge the pack track goes through decent swamp and coastal forest and climbs to a junction, one branch going to the tunnel and lookout. The tunnel was cut in the 1890s to avoid the awkward Gillespie Point headland.

Gillespies Lagoon

From here you can drop back down to the beach and walk 30 minutes to the fur seal colony at Galway Beach. It is mainly a resting colony during the non-breeding winter season, with up to 1500 seals. During the summer this drops to about 30-40 immature bull seals. Try not to disturb them, and if you are intending to go further north take the alternative inland track. The view from the trig is impressive, particularly if the nearby rata is flowering.

At the south carpark area at Gillespies, for about 3km you can follow on foot (it would be unwise to drive across the sandy gully) the rough vehicle track up onto Otorokua Head. Good views back to Gillespies and south to the Cook River wetland. There is also a small tidal lagoon at the south end of Gillespies Beach.

BLACK SANDING

The first finds of payable gold on the West Coast took place in river valleys. The discovery that the black beach sands were gold-rich was quite unexpected and led to extraordinary rushes at many beaches, most notably at the Three Mile and Five Mile (both just south of Okarito), with towns springing up overnight as the miners jostled and fought to be the first to peg out a claim. Some claims were spectacularly rich, with diggers washing several ounces of gold in a couple of hours. But new techniques had to be learned. The traditional sluicing box was put on wheels and pushed into the surf-line, where the pay dirt was shovelled onto the gold-tables and the ripple boards or linings separated the heavier gold from the lighter sand. Black-sand claims could be very quickly worked out – sometimes in a matter of hours. Storms did not help, washing in or taking out sand, and it was hard to predict where the good stuff would be. Once the first rush of miners had exhausted the obvious levels and leads there would always be a few 'hatters' left, solitary miners eking out a living, but no doubt enjoying the freedom and space of this glorious coast.

MONRO TRACK & SHIP CREEK

Features

South Westland beaches, Fiordland crested penguin, coastal forest and lagoons, pingao, rata forest, beach lookout.

Walking times

Monro Track 2-3 hours return, Ship Creek 1 hour return.

How to get there

For the Monro Track follow Highway 6 to Lake Moeraki Lodge and take the short side-road to the carpark and information signs. For Ship Creek drive south from Lake Moeraki another 9km. Ship Creek is about 10km north of Haast, with carpark, shelter, toilets, information signs and lookout tower.

These are two fine beaches only a few kilometres apart and both can be enjoyed in an afternoon. They are similar but different and the two illustrate much that is special and harsh about the South Westland coastal landscape.

At Ship Creek a small tidal stream twists down through pingao-topped sand to the plunging sea. Driftwood stands crouched and polished. A lone headland shuts off access north at high tide, and south there is a long beach – so long in fact that you can hardly make out where it ends. It goes virtually all the way to the Arawhata River and settlers used it for taking their cattle up to the markets in Hokitika. Behind you there is a sliver of sealed road, then dense rainforest with rimu trees notable at the road verges. The sea sound is constant and in the evenings the sunsets give a brilliant shine to the dark tidal creek.

The 'ship' has long been battered into nothingness. It was the stern of the *Schomberg*, which sank in Australia in 1855 and drifted right across the Tasman. Its disappearance says something about this wild shore – human endeavour is surprisingly impermanent.

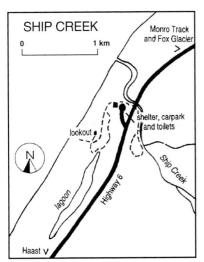

The walk illustrates the complexity of this coastal strip. The first plants to gain a foothold above the tide-line are small tussocks, such as the orange-red pingao, which help to establish the sands and enable such shrubs as flax to take hold. Pingao is unique to New Zealand and now becoming rare. The flax gives shelter for smaller tree shrubs, which get taller further back from the salt winds and meld into the rainforest itself. At Ship Creek the rainforest is dominated by old and twisted rata trees, with the kiekie vine winding around them in fantastic clumps.

107

KIEKIE

This coastal climber has heard many a swear word from travellers. It's odd that Europeans who usually always managed to find colloquial names for many obnoxious plants did not do so for kiekie – perhaps words failed them? Kiekie is a relative of the tropical pandanus, which manages to live in these southern frost-free coastal situations. It attaches itself to a holding tree and sends out a mass of aerial roots, forming large tangled clumps on the ground. It can grow profusely on coastal spurs and is rarely found far inland. The Maori still use the leaves for weaving, and the pulp of the ripe fruit used to be eaten once the bitter skin was removed.

The coastal lagoon has been trapped behind the dunes and provides a meeting ground for invertebrates and birds. Wood pigeons are common, as are the perky chaffinch and welcome swallow, which flit around the carpark.

Whatever you do, do not overlook the Swamp Walk. It is utter perfection.

Monro Track is a fine well-graded short walk that plunges the visitor into a thick forest of mixed podocarps and coastal plants such as the kiekie vine. The beach is sandy with the usual West Coast sea-rollers making it dangerous for swimming.

A colony of Fiordland crested penguins nest in the forest behind the northern part of Monro Beach, and people are requested not to pass beyond the penguin sign if they see birds on the beach.

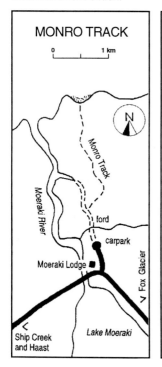

MONRO TRACK

0   1 km

Monro Track

Moeraki River

ford

carpark

Moeraki Lodge

Fox Glacier

Lake Moeraki

Ship Creek
and Haast

FIORDLAND CRESTED PENGUINS

It is sometimes hard to think of penguins as birds. They are superbly adapted to the sea, with their streamlined bodies and sleek, glossy feathers. They waddle comically across the open stretch of a beach such as Monro and no doubt feel uncomfortable on this exposed part of their daily ritual.

Fiordland crested penguins, one of the world's rarest birds, are strikingly attractive, with red beaks and a prominent yellow flash above the eye ending in a noticeable 'hair' tuft. They will climb up thick bush slopes to find a suitable nesting spot, under a fallen log for example, and return to the same place year after year. They lay two eggs in August-September and the young birds are fledged by November-December.

HAPUKA ESTUARY

Features
Estuary, kowhai coastal forest, whitebait.

Walking time
30 minutes.

How to get there
From Haast drive 15km down to Okuru (Haast Motor Camp). The walk is signposted 50m down a side-road. Carpark.

Estuaries are enormously productive places, and what looks like mud and sleaze to humans is a rich intermingling area of salt and fresh water, providing the nutrient base for plants and invertebrates that in turn attract birds. Hapuka is special because it demonstrates the whitebait story so well.

Whitebait are the young of five species of a native fish genus called galaxiids, of which the most prolific is the inanga. In autumn the female inanga lays eggs in the lower rivers and estuaries and the male releases milt to fertilise them. This milt can cloud the creeks. Most adult inanga then die but the eggs hatch into larvae and catch the big tides out to sea, where they live largely unknown lives. In spring the young fish (or whitebait) migrate back upriver, where the whitebaiter is waiting.

The crucial role of estuaries and wetlands as whitebait breeding areas is now only generally appreciated; destruction of the habitat by drainage and irrigation has seen whitebait become a treasured resource. The days when early travellers reported their dogs lapping out the whitebait are long gone, and the high excitement of the first

Whitebait

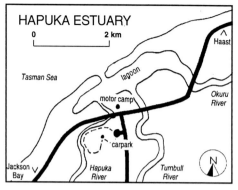

HAPUKA ESTUARY

0   2 km

Tasman Sea

lagoon

motor camp

Okuru
River

carpark

Jackson
Bay

Hapuka
River

Turnbull
River

Haast

N

whitebait catches of the season is matched by high prices in town. To think once whitebait were dumped as fertiliser!

The estuary track starts in the coastal kowhai forest, which grows on the work of other plants such as native broom (taineka), tutu and flax (harakeke), which have first fixed nitrogen from the air into the black river silts. Under the kowhai you get understorey plants such as manuka. Birds from normally different cultures mix together here: bush birds such as bellbirds, wood pigeons, tuis, yellow-breasted tomtits, grey warblers and fantails can be seen almost side by side with estuary-lovers such as oystercatchers (torea), bitterns (matuka), pukekos, and pied stilts (poaka).

In the waters there are eels (tuna), flounders (patiki), common bullies, and yellow-eyed mullets (aua), as well as mud crabs and mudflat snails (titiko).

After explaining the whitebait story the track leaves the estuary and wanders into a rich rimu forest with kiekie vine tangled through it, and there's an excellent lookout towards the two Open Bay Islands.

OPEN BAY ISLANDS

Taumaka and Popotai are two limestone islets that are still a Maori reserve, and were used for muttonbirding and gathering seabirds' eggs. They have some unusual features: no sandflies or mosquitoes, and a very rare type of land leech that is sanguivorous (blood-eating) and ornithophilous (bird-loving). The islands used to be home to numerous wetas, until wekas were introduced.

It's an important breeding place for fur seals and Fiordland crested penguins, and it was for the former that David Loweriston and his sealing crew were landed in 1810. The ship that was to pick them up got shipwrecked and for four years they survived on seal meat and a species of fern. They spent some time on the mainland but all their boat-building efforts were destroyed by storms. When they were eventually rescued they brought on board 11,000 cured seal skins.

OTAGO

Tidal pool

GRAVES WALKWAY

Features
Yellow-eyed penguins, little blue penguins, shag colony, pillow lava, shellfish, seals.

Walking time
2-3 hours return, but note that one section of the shoreline route needs a low tide to get past. There is a high-tide clifftop alternative track, but it's not that well marked in places and is at times barely more than a grassy trail that follows the fence-line. This may be upgraded in the future.

How to get there
From Oamaru take the Tyne Street Road, turning into Arun Street and Waterfront/ Breakwater Road. From there it is 1km to the carpark by the breakwater. The south access is along Tyne Street to the top of the hill, and then via Bushy Beach Road to the carpark and visitor centre.

The name Graves has nothing to do with cemeteries or funerals. The walkway was named after W. G. Grave, a man who mostly made his name in a number of daring and difficult traverses in the Milford Sound area of Fiordland – hence Grave-Talbot Pass, Mount Grave – but in later life became passionate about developing this lovely piece of coast as a walking track for locals to enjoy. At times he was literally cutting the track on his own, but with help from his friends and later from the council the walk was opened in the 1930s. Later it was lengthened around Cape Wenbrow to Bushy Beach.

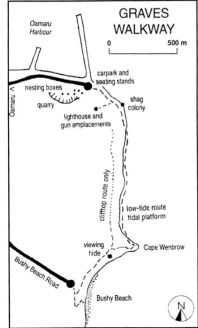

The track is well graded and starts from the wharf carpark. It neatly cuts around headlands, where native ice-plants tumble down the cliffs, as well as hebe and boxthorn. A perilous colony of pied shags perch underneath the track on the sea-cliffs – you can get a good view of them further along the track. A side-trail leads up to old gun emplacements and a lighthouse, and continues up to a look-out.

The main track drops down to a narrow sandy beach with intricate tidal platforms hosting a profusion of shellfish and seaweed. Pillow lava is visible at low tide, and the rocks are washed and eroded into striking patterns. Seals often haul out on the rocks, particularly around Cape Wenbrow.

After this low-tide stretch the track proper starts again on the headland at Cape Wenbrow and climbs sharply uphill to the grass-topped cliff and the lookout hide. This overlooks the orange sands of Bushy Beach, where both the little blue and the rare yellow-eyed penguin nest. The best time to watch for penguins is in the morning or late evening as they cross the sands. The birds will not usually come ashore if they see people on the beach so the hide is an excellent lookout.

The main track carries on to a junction, one branch climbing up the carpark at Bushy Beach Road and the other descending to the beach. Ngaio, flax, manuka and matipo (many of these planted as cover for the breeding penguins) give the slopes a forested effect. Shags can often be seen here, enjoying the seclusion of this coastal cove.

YELLOW-EYED PENGUINS – HOIHO

This is one of the rarest penguins in the world. Standing about 70cm high, with a striking band of yellow feathers around the eye and a yellow crown, the hoiho weighs 5-8 kilograms. They begin to breed in August-September, establishing a nest site quite high up under the coastal vegetation at Bushy Beach, and usually laying two eggs. They can nest up to 1km inland, but 500m is more usual. The young are independent after four months and the adults moult in February-March. Their calls are a loud screechy trumpeting, and one translation of hoiho is 'noisy'. Penguins eat a wide variety of fish and squid, and are in turn eaten by leopard seals and Hooker's sealions. The mortality rate of young hoiho at sea before breeding is 70-80 percent. They are vulnerable to disturbances throughout the breeding and moulting seasons, so follow the advice on the information boards and watch from a distance at the hide specially provided.

NIC BISHOP

NIC BISHOP

Little blue penguin

A viewing area and information office for little blue penguins (korara) has been established at the carpark at the start of the Graves Walkway. Seating stands have been set up, and road signs warn of penguins crossing. A charge is made. Every evening at dusk, particularly during the breeding months of August to December, bands of little blues clamber from the sea up the steep slopes of the wharf area and shuffle across to their burrows under the cliffs.

It is an endearing spectacle and voluntary wardens watch over this twilight return, keeping the public informed and preventing too much disturbance. Nesting burrows have been established in the quarry area, as well as native plantings to provide a more natural setting. Please do not use torches or camera flashes. Little blues are much smaller than the yellow-eyed penguins – about 25cm high and weighing about 1 kilogram. They usually lay two eggs and the chicks are independent after three months.

SHAG POINT

Features
Fur seals, shag colony, shore birds, tidal platform, historic mine.

Exploring time
1-2 hours.

How to get there
Just 10km south of the Moeraki Boulders (about 65km north of Dunedin) is the signposted turnoff to Shag Point. Follow the gravel road past the bach community into the various carparking areas that occupy the headland of Shag Point itself.

Shag Point is a small low headland that was once the site of one of Otago's largest coalmines, with half a million tons of coal extracted from undersea coal shafts from the 1860s to the 1980s. At one time in the 1880s over 170 people were employed and a short railway line linked Shag Point with the main trunk line. Now hardly a trace remains except a concrete air-vent on the headland and large mullock heaps of rock and tailings slightly inland.

What is amazing is that through all this disturbance the fur seals kept returning to bask on the rocks, the shags kept breeding on their islet, and the yellow-eyed penguins made their dangerous dash to and from their inland nest sites. Perhaps the miners were too busy to bother the wildlife.

Wild things have been coming to Shag Point for a long time. A fossil plesiosaur, a large marine reptile thought to be between 65 and 135 million years old, was found in a cretaceous concretion at Shag Point. This toothed predator was 7m long and would have made diving interesting. The mudstone platform also contains fossils of gastropods and bivalves as well as traces of trees and leaves.

At first sight Shag Point might seem disappointing (after all, you can drive round most of it) but once you start exploring, the beauty of the place becomes apparent. Massive tidal platforms are exposed at low tide and shags flap vigorously along the coastal edge, rarely more than 30m above your head, as they return to the crowded and squabbling colony on the offshore islet. There are several tiny and pretty sandy coves, and fur seals loll about in lots of unexpected places – the smell usually gives their presence away.

KELP

There are two main seaweeds at Shag Point: bull kelp flourishes in the immediate 'battle zone' of sea and rocks, and bladder or giant kelp grows further out. Bull kelp has broad strands (straps) and grows widely around New Zealand coasts. It can grow up to 10m long and live up to 10 years. The yellow foot or 'holdfast' is often seen rotting on beaches. A honeycomb of air spaces in the straps keeps the bull kelp buoyant and allows it to tolerate wave impact so that it acts as a buffer between the sea and rocks and, from a human perspective, helps to reduce coastal erosion. There are two species of bull kelp on mainland New Zealand. Both are slow growers, adding perhaps 3m in two years.

Bladder kelp, on the other hand, is reckoned to be the world's fastest-growing plant, sometimes putting on as much as 50cm a day! Since it is usually sited in less disturbed waters it can grow up to 30m long and, as the name suggests, it gets its buoyancy from little air bladders that kids delight in popping when they find them cast up on shore.

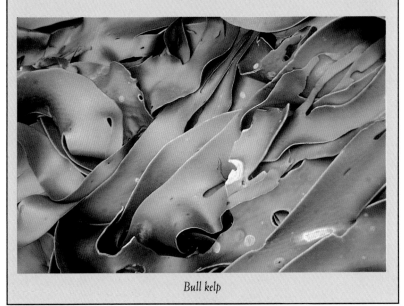

Bull kelp

The rocks and tidal platforms around Shag Point have been worn and chiselled into many different patterns, with several Moeraki-like concretions. However, these katiki concretions tend to erode from the inside out and there are many stages of this process arrayed attractively on the low-tide rocks.

SANDFLY BAY

Features
Fur seals, sand dunes, yellow-eyed penguins.

Walking time
2-3 hours return.

How to get there
About 18km from Dunedin take the Highcliff Road on Otago Peninsula (towards Larnach's castle) and follow it to Pukehiki. There is a side-road to a small carpark at the road end. Signposted.

This is an enchanting place and typical of the glories of Otago Peninsula. The peninsula has stony or pebbly beaches on the harbour side and large secluded sandy beaches on the seaward side. Victory Beach, Allan's Beach, Tomahawk Beach, St Clair and the misnamed Boulder Beach are all worthy of inspection.

Dunedin touts itself as the wildlife capital of New Zealand and for once the tourist tag is true. There are yellow-eyed penguins nesting on the peninsula's lonely beaches, albatrosses at Taiaroa Head, fur seals hauling out on the rock shores, and sealions beaching in lazy clumps. Pilot whales sometimes come right into Otago harbour. This wildlife was always there, of course – it's just that now humans have started to take notice.

To get to Sandfly Bay from the carpark follow the steep farm track towards the bay and romp down a big sand dune to the wide spacious beach flats. Black

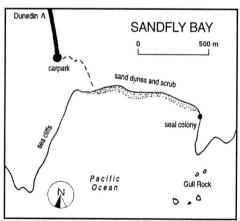

headlands trap the bay and wind scours these flats into intricate and attractive patterns. On the rocks at the north end there is a small non-breeding colony of fur seals which, though apparently lazy, always keep one wary liquid eye on intruders. Yellow-eyed penguins nest in the dunes at the back of the beach and people should take particular care not to disturb any nesting or moulting birds.

ALBATROSSES (AND OTHER WILD THINGS)

At Taiaroa Head is the famous albatross colony – the only mainland breeding colony of albatrosses in the world. These gentle giants (toroa) with their 3m-plus wingspan use the updraughts of Taiaroa Head to launch themselves on their long solo flights. Several chicks are raised every year, but these can be seen only by doing an organised tour. The information centre is well laid out and worth a look even if you don't want to pay to see the big birds.

You can still see free wildlife at Taiaroa Head. From the carpark you can walk down to the cliff-edge lookout, where you can watch the alarming flights of the shags as they spin and gyrate towards their cliffside nesting colonies. You can also often get a grandstand view of an albatross itself as it soars along the cliff faces. Down at Pilot Bay (on the side-road) there is a pleasant picnic area and a fenced-off seal colony that usually has a few fur seals lazing about. Sometimes the younger seals get quite curious and come along to the public side to inspect the visitors. Little blue penguins also nest in the light shrubbery around Pilot Bay.

Also on the peninsula is a guided tour to a yellow-eyed penguin colony. Penguin Place is a serious attempt to show visitors these impressive birds at close quarters while also helping the penguins breed. Nesting boxes are provided and a close eye is kept on potential predators.

The Dunedin Information Centre will give you information and prices for the albatross colony and Penguin Place.

Friendly seal at Pilot Bay

TUNNEL BEACH

Features
Coastal sea-cliffs and views, archway, tunnel.

Walking time
2 hours return.

How to get there
From Dunedin follow Highway 1 over the first hill out of town down towards Green Island, then turn onto the Green Island Bush Road across Blackhead Road to the small carpark (6km from the Octagon). Take care not to block the turning area for other users. The track is closed from August to October.

A fine short walk to a powerful carved coastline of arches, sea-stacks and sandstone cliffs.

From the carpark the track crosses paddocks and then follows a vehicle track down through sheep-grazed slopes dotted with gorse clumps – bright yellow in spring. The coastline of Tunnel Beach is vividly and immediately visible. The rock here is called Caversham sandstone, a soft sediment laid down over the Dunedin area about 20 million years ago. At Otago Peninsula the sandstone got smothered with lava from later volcanic activity, but at Tunnel Beach this did not happen and it's still possible to detect fossil fragments in the cliffs from those ancient times.

The track wanders onto the top of a sandstone platform that has its own arch cut underneath. Take great care here because there are no restraining fences and children should be watched carefully. The sea surges through the archway and bashes into the coves where large blocks of sandstone have been cut under and fallen in. Eventually the archway will be eroded out completely, collapse and form a sea-stack, a sort of mini-island. Several other sea stacks can be seen along this rugged coastline.

On top of the platform only the hardiest plant survives the combination of salt spray, sheep intrusion and human feet. It is likely that in the future some system of boardwalks may have to be built to reduce the effects of human visitors. Both black-backed and red-billed gulls make their presence obvious, as do the pigeons that find strategic nesting strongholds on some of the sheer pinnacles of sandstone.

TUNNEL BEACH

0   500 m

Dunedin
carpark
sea cliffs
tunnel
Tunnel Beach
sea cliffs
archway
N

GORSE

This is not a popular plant. Gorse was exported to New Zealand largely as a good hedging shrub. Unfortunately it grew to super-strength proportions in New Zealand's benevolent climate and quickly got out of control, and it is now one of the country's most widespread and visible shrubs. It's not even very good for hedging because it grows too spindly.

Gorse loves open spaces and grows where the native forest has been cleared off. It is extremely tenacious and its seeds will survive repeated burn-offs. Ironically, conservationists have found that in certain conditions gorse can provide a screen for native species regenerating underneath, which will in turn force their way through the gorse canopy, slowly outgrowing and removing it. This succession has been particularly noticeable in urban areas such as the Hutt Valley and on the Rimutaka Hill near Wellington.

NIC BISHOP

Now for the tunnel. Concrete steps have been laid down as the tunnel drops steeply some 50m to the tiny bay. The tunnel was built in the 1870s for the Cargills, a wealthy Dunedin family (as in Cargill's castle), to supply an exclusive and private beach for the children. Swimming here is not particularly safe and at high tide the beach can feel uncomfortably small, but at low tide this is a strangely charming spot – threatening and church-like at the same time. The cliffs have fluted rock buttresses and incised clefts but unfortunately the soft sandstone has been liberally vandalised with graffiti.

It's a slow 150m trudge back up to the clifftop and carpark but it's worth lingering over the views along the coast, particularly in the late evening light, as the colours illuminate the seascape.

SUTTON SALT LAKE

Features
Salt lake and salt plants, rock outcrops.

Walking time
The full circuit takes 1-2 hours return.

How to get there
From Dunedin take Highway 87 for 76km towards Sutton, then turn down Kidds Road 2km to the signposted carpark.

This curious lakelet is in the heart of Central Otago, a vast Old Testament landscape of arid tussock hills and rock outcrops that stare like faces. Puffy cumulus clouds appear to come close to the earth here because so little intrudes between the eye and the sky.

Central Otago could be called a sort of desert. Geologically it is a huge eroded plain that can only be really appreciated from the air, where myriad creeks have cut slots into the plateaus, forming larger rivers that sometimes become so uncertain in direction that they used to make huge swamp wetlands – now mostly drained or dammed. Areas such as the Great Moss Swamp seem almost a contradiction in the dry regions of Central, famous for its frosts in winter and intense heat in summer.

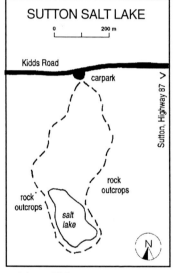

The Sutton Salt Lake is an oddity in many ways. Natural lakes are in any case rare in Central, but here the rain running through the rocks and soil has concentrated minute quantities of dissolved salts, producing a lake that is about half as salty as seawater. The plants have had to respond to this, so you have the curious situation of salt-tolerant coastline plants fringing the lake.

Some argue that the lake was once – millions of years ago – part of an old coastline. This would help explain the presence of the salt-adapted creatures, and perhaps the salt weathering from the landscape maintained this little lake. In any case, Sutton Lake is New Zealand's only inland salt lake.

The salt-friendly plants consist of the small fleshy-leaved and ground-hugging *Lilaeopsis*, and another ground-lying plant, *Selliera*. There is also a common saltmarsh glasswort. There are no fish in the lake (which can seasonally dry up), but there are copepods, salt-adapted aquatic animals. Skinks and geckos can be found within the reserve, as well as invertebrates such as a tussock butterfly and cicada. Several bird species visit, notably the noisy paradise shelduck, black swan, mallard duck, shoveller duck, pied oystercatcher, harrier, the occasional falcon and the white-faced heron.

Tussock landscape, Central Otago

As the walking track meanders around the lake it seems that the lake itself is less of a feature than the dramatic schist tors that are so characteristic of Central Otago. The huge weathering process does its work unevenly and some schist rocks resist better than others – hence these columnar tors. In misty weather they can look like giants that have lost their way. Lichens have seized a hold on the rocks, creating some striking colours across the brooding, almost sinister tors.

SKINKS

If you see a flash of black and gold colour on a rock then you might have seen a skink. The Otago skink and grand skink (each measuring about 30cm) inhabit the rock crevices in the schist outcrops and tors, and both are jet black with yellow and gold markings, which acts as an excellent camouflage among the lichen-covered rocks. Grand skinks are more active and alert than the more sedate Otago skinks, which like to bask in family groups within easy reach of a safe crevice. Both are found mainly in the Middlemarch and Macraes Flat area, and there are also populations in the Lindis Pass region.

ROXBURGH GORGE

Features
Rocky gorge, Clutha River and lake, Chinese rock shelters, historic goldmining sites.

Walking time
To Coleman's Creek return allow 3-4 hours. It is wise to carry some water as it is not easy to get through the scrub to the Clutha, and the gorge can get intensely hot in summer.

How to get there
From Alexandra it's about a 1km walk from the post office to the historic Shaky Bridge (built in 1877), then a 2km walk to the Graveyard Gully cemetery.

If you are driving, take the road towards the famous hillside clock and lookout, turn right after crossing the Manuherikia and follow the gravel road to the carpark and signposts.

This landscape is dry, harsh, forbidding – not everyone's cup of tea. The browned rocky slopes of the gorge hold a deep silence that even the slickly moving Clutha River does not disturb. Central Otago is often characterised as a desert landscape, and the rainfall around Lake Roxburgh is less than 350mm (13-14 inches) per year.

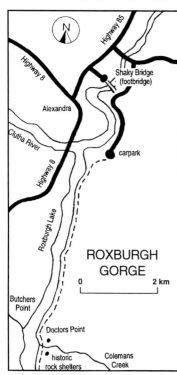

It is a parched landscape and, to many visitors, unbelievably hostile.

The 'river' is actually part of a hydro lake, dammed almost 30km below Alexandra at the town of Roxburgh, and the absence of river noise only heightens the sound of a few pairs of paradise shelducks, whose calls echo mournfully off the escarpments.

It would have taken a powerful reason for humans to come here, and the reason was gold. From the late 1850s prospectors fossicked through the Clutha Valley, and in the Roxburgh Gorge (as in many places) gold was extracted in several stages. First amateur diggers worked all the easy gold, sluicing where possible and 'crevicing' in winter, when the low river levels allowed them to reach exposed rocks in the riverbed and tease out gold trapped in the crevices.

After the European diggers came the more frugal Chinese, who reworked old ground, recovering gold through painstaking methods. It was the Chinese who built many of the rock shelters, cleverly utilising

Track, Roxburgh Gorge   *Wild thyme*

the natural 'plateyness' of the schist rock, first for overhangs and then for building bricks, with mud as cement. There's a three-roomed shelter at Coleman's Creek called 'Mary Ann's' after the last Chinese miner in the area. Once the easiest gold was exhausted, larger companies brought in sluicing guns and gold dredges and bridle tracks on either side of the gorge were built in the 1890s to supply the first dredges. Finally, there was a period during the Depression of the 1930s when the government subsidised relief schemes that saw about 80 miners working at Doctor's Point.

The walk to Coleman's Creek shows traces of the gold days. Here and there are rock shelters, there's a large hut at Coleman's Creek (Leaky Lodge), and there are obvious sluice workings. In order to obtain enough water pressure, water was taken from Butcher's Creek opposite, and ingeniously carried over the Clutha by a suspended pipeline.

The striking feature of the gorge walk is the barrenness of the landscape and the success of the introduced plants. Willows by the waterside, lupins higher up, some red-berry briar, broom, occasional poplars and, higher up the hillside, 'wilding' conifers that are slowly self-seeding the dry slopes. Everywhere there is thyme, with its aromatic smell (one pamphlet calls it a roast duck smell!) and small pretty pink and white flowers in spring. Of the introduced birds, yellowhammers are obvious, as are chaffinches and some song thrushes. Pipits and paradise ducks are the most noticeable native species.

It is worth just stopping and listening to the silence. The river-lake sometimes emits sinister gurgles, and both bumble-bees and honey-bees love the thyme and

NIC BISHOP

RAPTORS

Raptors are birds of prey. New Zealand has only two: the endemic falcon and the Australasian harrier hawk (kahu, above). The falcon, a fierce independent bird that on attack can reach speeds of 200 kilometres an hour, is becoming rare. It is mainly in the high country and mountainlands of the South Island, prefers nesting in trees or rocky ledges, and has a distinctive 'kek-kek' call. The harrier hawk is much more common – it's the one you see on the roadside pecking away at a dead possum. Larger than the falcon, the harrier is also a solitary hunter, although as many as 50 birds will group together in autumn and winter. The harrier prefers to roost on the ground in swamplands. Both raptors hunt during the day, feeding mainly on dead and small animals such as mice, frogs, rats and some rabbits and small birds. Both can occasionally be seen in the clear air over the Roxburgh Gorge: elegant in the updraughts, terrible in descent.

provide a constant background droning. Skinks might be spotted slithering in a flash under rocks or shrub cover. Remember the diggers, who worked in either the intense dry heat of summer or the bitter sub-zero days of winter. The first moment of winter sun to creep into the sunless gorge must have been like a flash of gold to them.

CATLINS COAST

Hooker's sealion

NUGGET POINT

Features
Rock islets, fur seals, sea elephants, Hooker's sealions, yellow-eyed penguins, leopard seals.

Walking time
20 minutes return to the lighthouse, 15 minutes return to Roaring Bay.

How to get there
From Highway 92 turn off at Romahapa (16km south of Balclutha) and drive to Kaka Point, then follow the coast road past Willsher Bay to Roaring Bay and Nugget Point carparks. The last part of the road is narrow.

Nugget Point is a finger-like promontory that juts out from the Catlins coast and ends in a muddle of rock platforms and wind-battered islets – the sort of place that the early settlers regarded with suspicion: no use for farming, dangerous for fishing and a hazard for ships (there are many wrecks recorded here). So they built a lighthouse, which became automatic in 1989, and left Nugget Point alone.

It is this isolation that enabled the unique wildlife to stay relatively undisturbed, for this is the only place in New Zealand where elephant seals breed, and is a known haul-ashore point for Hooker's sealions and breeding place for fur seals and yellow-eyed penguins.

The short walk from the carpark is wonderful, following a narrow path on the peninsula to the lighthouse and viewing platform. Access beyond here is steep and slippery and is not advised: take a pair of binoculars instead. There's a small colony of red-billed gulls and black-backed gulls, and a pair of binoculars can track the impressive ease with which they catch the crosswinds and updraughts off the stacks. The sooty shearwater or muttonbird (titi) colonies are one of the largest on the mainland. There are roosting colonies of spotted shags, and the Stewart Island shag visits the rocks to sun and preen. Many of the islets have Maori names: Te Anau Putu, 'the islet with the sea cave'; Pae Koua, 'perch of the shag'; Makanui, 'seals'; and Porokaua, 'the furthest stack'.

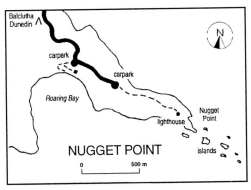

NUGGET POINT

Up to 60 fur seal pups are born here each year in a colony of up to 500 seals, and there are usually plenty of seals to look at. The seals have made tracks all over the rock jumble on the platform, even on some of the steepest scarps, and the pups as well as adults seem quite non-chalant as they negotiate steep rocks.

129

NIC BISHOP

ELEPHANT SEALS

The enormous elephant seals are most likely to be seen from mid-October to late November in the deep kelp channels they use as access to a cavern below the lighthouse, and again from January to March when they return to moult. The main elephant seal breeding grounds are on Campbell and Macquarie islands, so this small mainland breeding colony is unique. The distinctive nose of the elephant seal is believed to be a resonating chamber, which presumably increases the bull's roar when competing for females. The huge male seals can weigh up to three tonnes and dive to depths of 1200m.

Hooker's sealions come ashore on the rocks all year round, as do occasional leopard seals.

At Roaring Bay there is a viewing hide overlooking a small breeding colony of yellow-eyed penguins, which nest in the low forest and scrub, often quite high up. The best time to see the world's rarest penguin is early morning when they go out to feed, or late in the evening when they return. The penguins are easily disturbed and will not venture onto the beach if they see humans, so take binoculars and keep a discreet distance. Moulting in February and April is a particularly vulnerable time since they cannot swim to escape.

You can walk to the small southern headland which at low tide has a pretty double sea-arch drilled through it. There's a chance you might spot Hooker's sealions basking on the stones and also New Zealand fur seals, which loll about in the kelp and tidal platforms around the headland. Sealions are generally less wary than fur seals but can become aggressive if approached too closely.

CANNIBAL BAY

Features
Coastal sand and sandhills, moa-hunter
sites, tidal platforms, Hooker's sealions.

Walking time
The walk to Surat Bay and back takes about
1-2 hours. From Cannibal Bay to the Surat

Bay road end allow 2-3 hours.

How to get there
2km north of Owaka on Highway 92 turn
onto the signposted Cannibal Bay road for
9km to the small carpark and picnic area by
the beach.

Cannibal Bay and Surat Bay are two wide sandy beaches separated by sand dunes
and a headland called False Islet. Surat got its unusual name from the French ship
that was wrecked here in 1874, and Cannibal Bay goes back to the time when the
Maori occupied sites among the sand dunes, and there is evidence of moa-hunting.
People are asked not to disturb these sites.

Cannibal Bay is the smaller and prettier, about 1km long, with a fascinating
tidal platform at the east end at low tide. The rocks have been etched into 'railway
tracks', long straight layers of sandstone that were tilted and later exposed, with
the harder types of sandstone standing proud. Bull kelp has attached itself firmly
to the rocks by means of its rock-like yellow foot (or 'holdfast') and the usual
oystercatchers and gulls hover around the rocks.

In the sand dunes behind the beach yellow-eyed penguins come in to nest and
sometimes you can spot their characteristic waddling footprints in the sands.
Morning and evening are the best times to see them.

At the other end of Cannibal Bay (the south side) a signposted track leads
through the extensive sand dune area which hardly looks a sheltered place in a

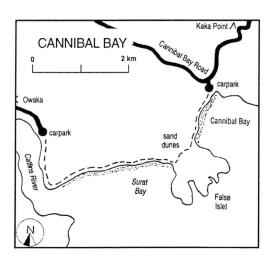

Tidal platform, Cannibal Bay

SEALIONS

The name sealion is a tribute to the light 'mane' on the bull sealions; another European nickname was 'hair seals'. The bulls can weigh up to 400kg, and if disturbed get up on their front flippers and strut their stuff with loud aggressive snorts, their pink mouths contrasting with their shiny black-brown bodies. Female sealions weigh only 150kg and are paler and less aggressive. The main sealion colonies are in the subantarctic Auckland islands (the main breeding areas), but they are slowly returning in greater numbers to the Catlins coast and Otago Peninsula. There is some early evidence that they may be starting to breed on the mainland again, after being slaughtered by Maori and European sealers. But they are easily disturbed and it's essential that we give them proper space if we want them continue to visit our shores.

storm. Trail-bikes have made a bit of a mess in some areas of the dunes – they are not permitted of course, but that never stopped a trail-biker. The track leads across the base of False Islet and reaches the south end of the lovely Surat Beach, 3km or so of yellow sand.

On both Cannibal Bay and Surat Bay there is certainly a chance of seeing bull sealions, particularly during spring, where they like to gather and bask on the warm sands or in the dunes behind. On hot days they often flick sand over their black bodies and could be mistaken for a large lump of driftwood – so be careful! At the south end of Surat Bay there is another jagged tidal platform to explore.

CURIO BAY

Features

Fossilised forest, tidal platforms, Hector's dolphins.

Walking time

1 hour.

How to get there

Curio Bay is 88km from Invercargill off Highway 92, via either Otara or the slightly more direct Waikawa. Well signposted. There is a camping ground on the headland (toilets, water, store in season) that must have one of the best outlooks in New Zealand.

Curio Bay is a peaceful spot. Headlands enclose rock platforms that are home to dozens of species of marine fauna.

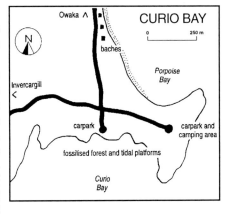

Like most of the Catlins coast Curio Bay gets its share of wildlife visitors. There are fur seals on the rocky shores, Hector's dolphins in nearby Porpoise Bay, and shags, white-faced herons, oystercatchers and seagulls. The tidal platform is fascinating, with a surprising range of colours and rock structures. Bleached seaweed, small natural salt pans, and zillions of tiny shellfish that crunch under your feet. There's a striking contrast between the gnarly rock platform of Curio Bay and the smooth sweep of sand in Porpoise Bay, with just five minutes separating the two very different environments.

But what is distinctive about Curio Bay is that its funny black 'rocks' are actually fossilised tree stumps from one of the most extensive and least disturbed fossil forests in the world. The violent processes that brought the trees to this state and left them beached on the remote and tranquil Catlins coast were complex.

HECTOR'S DOLPHINS

These are the smallest members of the dolphin family, about 135cm long and unique to New Zealand. They have attractive black and white patterning and a rounded dorsal fin that is an obvious identification point. With an estimated population of only 3000-4000, Hector's are under intensive study with a view to their protection and preservation. Groups of Hector's are common in Curio Bay. They are interested in humans and will leap and surf around boats and play with pieces of seaweed.

Fossilised forest tree stumps, Curio Bay

The fossilised forest has a history that goes back to Gondwanaland. About 180 million years ago this ancient super-continent comprised much of Antarctica, Australia, Africa, India and South America. Curio Bay forest then would have looked like much New Zealand rainforest today – luxuriant ferns and trees such as kauri and matai. There were a few dinosaurs but no birds, and much of modern New Zealand at that time was under water.

Volcanic activity repeatedly buried the forest with ash, then new forest would grow, to be followed by another reburial. This happened at least four times, until the sediments were buried deeply and silica minerals invaded the woody tree stumps, quite literally turning them to stone. Finally, the rock was brought to the surface and eroded by the sea to expose the fossilised tree stumps.

WAKATIPU & SOUTHLAND

Mistletoe — pirita

BLUE POOL

Features
Beech forest, bush birds.

Walking time
30-50 minutes return.

How to get there
From Wanaka drive on Highway 6 past Makarora about 65km to the signposted carpark.

This is a lovely walk down through mature silver beech forest to the Makarora and Blue rivers. The forest is unbelievably lush, filling every nook and cranny of the forest. Keep an eye out for the unique strawberry fungus, a small honeycombed yellow ball that grows only on silver beech branches and drops off

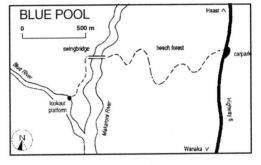

to the base of the tree. Several plaques identify different tree species. Birdlife is vocal, with tuis, bellbirds and wood pigeons frequently heard.

Silver beech forest

There is a long swingbridge over the Makarora and the track sidles around to a platform that overlooks the Blue River as it bustles out of its gorge and settles in a deep aquamarine pool. A side-track also goes down to the riverbed.

POSSUMS

NIC BISHOP

The brushtail possum (not opossum) is probably now New Zealand's number one pest in native forests. The numbers of deer, another forest pest, were drastically reduced in the 1970s and are likely to remain manageable because they are still a sought-after game species. Rats and the mustelids (stoats, weasels and ferrets) still eat alarming numbers of native bird eggs and chicks but at least they don't eat the forest as well. Possums have had a devastating effect on native forests, particularly the rata-kamahi forests on the West Coast, which in some places have turned from green to grey.

Possums were introduced from Australia by acclimatisation societies and enjoyed some legal protection up to 1947. They are selective eaters, with a hierarchy of favourite plants – fuchsia, rata, kamahi, wineberry and five-finger are some of the most favoured. They first strip one tree, then move on to the next, and once the favourite trees have been exhausted they shift to the next-preferred plants such as totara, tawa and mahoe. They dislike being wet so rivers are natural barriers. Generally possums are solitary, except for mating, and usually live for up to five years.

Possums have no natural enemies in New Zealand, so as they merrily munch their way through the forest they have managed to reach a population of 70 million. Possums also carry bovine tuberculosis, which poses a serious threat to any cattle that investigate dead possums in paddocks. But by far the most sinister threat has emerged recently with videotaped evidence of possums eating kokako eggs, and possibly even chicks, raising the concern that possums may predate on a wide range of different native birds.

So forget the cute and cuddly image – possum fur is in.

LAKE ALTA

Features
Alpine mountains and lake, alpine wetland and flowers.

Walking time
3 hours return to Lake Alta. This walk is strictly a summer and fair-weather trip.

How to get there
From Queenstown drive to Frankton and then down Highway 6 to the turnoff to the Remarkables Ski-field and Rastus Recreation Reserve (9km). This road is open in summer and climbs 6km to just over 1500m and the main carpark by the facilities base. Although it is a wide and well-graded road, washouts and slips can occur and drivers should take care at all times. Downhill traffic traditionally gives way to uphill.

There are few places in New Zealand where you can drive with such ease to such a magnificent setting. The views on the way up are impressive as you glance over Lake Hayes and the rival ski-field of Coronet Peak, and up to Mount Earnslaw and Mount Aspiring. Then the road turns into the valley of the Rastus Burn to the strangely empty ski-field. At this time of year the T-bars are silent and the base locked up; virtually the only sounds are the wind in the giant pylons and the gurgle of the Rastus Burn as it leaves Lake Alta and rushes down the valley.

In winter this is a snow scene, packed with people, noise and bright colours. The summer scene is more subtle: yellowing tussocks, red lichen-stained rocks, white flowering daisies, and the sounds of a kea or a lone hectoring seagull.

It is about a 200m climb from the carpark to Lake Alta. Follow the easy vehicle track around the ski-field buildings until it crosses the Rastus Burn to the track start.

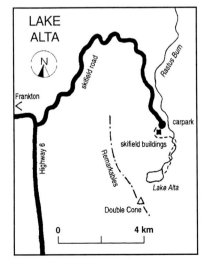

Interpretation signs and cairns mark the track but at present it is not poled.

This alpine wetland is very fragile, and wherever possible people should keep to the track and walk on the rocks rather than the moss. One hefty footprint can damage a lot of plants. Get down to the plant's eye level and marvel at the complexity of alpine mosses and flowers in a single square metre. Some of the cushion plant flowers measure only a millimetre across!

The trail follows the Rastus Burn and crosses it occasionally. Interpretation signs explain the graduations of plant habitat, from alpine wetlands to fellfields and cushion plant environments, to the harsh rock fields themselves.

NIC BISHOP

VEGETABLE SHEEP

This curious cushion plant earns its name from some of the larger specimens that from a distance an exhausted musterer once mistook for the woolly humps of his stray sheep. Here the vegetable sheep are quite small and survive among a number of different cushion plants that have all perfected similar mechanisms for surviving at these altitudes. Wiry, tough branches, with densely packed leaves at the tip to reduce wind battering, fleshy or hairy leaves that trap moisture and slow evaporation, and an internal self-mulching network of dead leaves and branches. Cushion species often buttress against each to prevent other plants from shading them, and so manage to survive in a remarkably hostile and unforgiving landscape.

In fine weather it is a straightforward walk up to a viewpoint that overlooks the eye-blue of the lake, trapped in a circle of splintered mountains. There will still be some snow among the dark gullies and numerous pinnacles of the Remarkables. The highest peak is Double Cone (2324m).

The most likely bird you will see and hear is the pipit, but seagulls, keas, paradise ducks and pied oystercatchers make abrupt appearances. What attracts them is the insect life, which with cicadas, butterflies, moths, a giant 2-3cm weevil and several species of grasshopper provides a good food source. Cave wetas have been found in the rocks above Lake Alta.

BOB'S COVE

Features
Lake views, red beech forest, old lime kilns, historic bridle track.

Walking time
Nature walk to Bob's Cove and peninsula lookout 1 hour return; to Twelve Mile Bluff 1 hour return; to Twelve Mile Creek delta 2 hours return.

How to get there
From Queenstown take the Glenorchy Road for 14km to the Twelve Mile Creek delta, or 1km further to the small signposted carpark. Camping area with toilets at the delta, great views. The access road to the Twelve Mile Creek delta is quite steep.

The southern lakes are an impressive feature of the lower South Island – Tekapo, Pukaki, Ohau, Hawea, Wanaka, Wakatipu, Te Anau and Manapouri. There are also lakes that humans have added to the menage, such as Benmore and, recently, Lake Dunstan.

Wakatipu is New Zealand's third largest lake: 84km long and 5km at its widest, with consistent depth of about 370m. The lake is used for access and transport, irrigation, power generation and of course leisure and recreation. Bob's Cove, named after Bob Fortune, a boatman back in the 1870s, was a popular picnic place for the ladies and gentlemen of the 1880s and has not lost its popularity.

From the carpark at Bob's Cove there are several walk options. There is a short loop along a nature trail to the lakeside and through native forest, with bellbirds, song

---

SEICHES

This strange-sounding word refers to the natural phenomenon of fluctuations in the lake water level due to variations in atmospheric pressure. It has been likened to a beating heart and is common to most large lakes. In the case of Lake Wakatipu there is a seiche along the length of the lake (taking about 50 minutes for a complete oscillation), and a seiche across the breadth of the lake (taking about 4-5 minutes). Bob's Cove is a good place to observe the seiche phenomenon, simply by placing a stick in the water at a sheltered point.

The Maori had a more poetic explanation for the seiche. The full name for the lake was Wakatipuawaimaori ('waka' canoe or trough; 'tipua' enchanted being; 'wai maori' fresh water: 'trough of fresh water where the giant lies'), and there is a story about a giant that had stolen a beautiful girl. As the giant slept, with his knees drawn up, the girl's lover crept up and set fire to his bed of ferns. Soon the giant was overcome by the smoke and the fat from his enormous body burnt furiously so his body sank, forming the trough where the lake lies. His heart was the only part of the giant not reduced to ashes and keeps beating still, causing the mysterious rise and fall of the water.

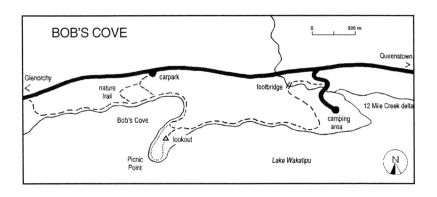

BOB'S COVE

Glenorchy
<
nature
trail

carpark

footbridge

Queenstown
>

12 Mile Creek delta

Bob's Cove

camping
area

△ lookout

Picnic
Point

Lake Wakatipu

N

NIC BISHOP

Silvereye

thrushes, silvereyes, fantails, chaffinches, shining cuckoos (in season) and grey warblers providing an accompaniment.

By continuing towards Twelve Mile Bluff you plunge into some old and impressive red beech forest, and nature signs illustrate plants such as fuchsia and lancewood. This track follows the old bridle trail to Twelve Mile Bluff, which was opened up by gold diggers in the 1870s and later became a stock route.

The alternative is to follow the lapping foreshore of the cove (past good picnic sites) around to the old lime kilns. In the 1870s and 80s limestone was quarried from the area and turned into slack lime by a slow burning process – about 70 hours for each kiln-load. The lime was used as a building mortar. Sandstone was also quarried here for making into gravestones.

Further round there is an old jetty where pied shags sun themselves on the wood piles. It's well worthwhile following the track to the top of the small peninsula called Picnic Point, with excellent views of Wakatipu, the Remarkables and Walter Peak. The track around the peninsula is becoming a bit overgrown and unclear in places.

A longer walk goes east some 3km to the Twelve Mile Creek delta. The track goes down to the lakeside a few times but mostly stays high on a terrace where there is a curious mixture of eucalyptus, manuka, broom, gorse and lancewood. The eucalypts were apparently planted for firewood by the lime company. Eventually the track reaches the delta, swings around and crosses Twelve Mile Creek a little upstream, over a pretty gorge.

MAVORA LAKES

Features
Alpine lakes, beech forest, bush birds, tussock valleys.

Walking time
3-4 hours return around South Mavora Lake. Mavora Walkway 2-3 days. North Mavora Lake edge 4-5 hours return.

How to get there
From Highway 94 about 30km west of Mossburn, follow the unsealed road for 40km to the South Mavora Lake. There are many camping and picnic areas, with toilets and barbecue sites at both the South and North Mavora lakes.

Mavora Lakes is the sort of place Kiwi families go to. Pack up the caravan, load the kids in, drive to a campsite (probably the same one you've had for the last 10 years), put up the massive tent, get out the gas burner and have a whole two weeks of chats, fishing and cups of tea. Your tent neighbours are probably the same as last year's, the stories improve with age and everyone comes back chronically sunburnt – except for the kids, who have managed to attain an all-over tan, even underneath their arms. So perhaps high summer is not the ideal time to go to Mavora Lakes, but for 11 months of the year the Mararoa Valley is quiet and forgotten, and in midwinter the beech trees around the lakes are beautiful under layers of deepening frost.

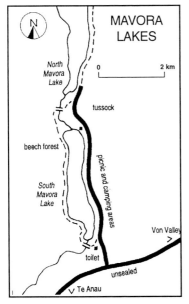

The road gives access to both lakes, the South Mavora being smaller and more attractive. There is a short 1km gap before the much larger North Mavora Lake, where power boating is allowed. The fishing season is October to April.

The best walk is to cross the long swingbridge at the foot of the South Mavora Lake and follow the lakeside around to the deep green pool in the river outlet from the North Mavora. Here, another swingbridge takes you back to the road, which you can follow back to your car. The walk is through quiet beech forest with a healthy variety of bush birds, including the rifleman, parakeet, yellow-breasted tomtit and the ever-inquisitive robin. On the lake there are various ducks, including common mallards and the mournful-sounding paradise ducks. Brown trout and rainbow trout break the still surface of the lake.

TUSSOCK

Anyone who has passed over the Lindis Pass in late evening or early morning and watched the blending colours of gold and pink, softened by the tussocks into almost human forms, is aware that tussock is not just a 'grass'. Tussocks are the dominant plant species in the South Island high country – 3 million hectares or some 10 per cent of New Zealand's land area – and form an indispensable part of New Zealand's landscape. They epitomise space and freedom.

They have adapted to the harsh conditions of the high country and can cope with strong winds, extreme drought and cold, fire and snow. Yet tussock grasslands are visually subtle, fragile and easily damaged by humans.

There are several tussock species. Slim snow tussock is dominant north of the Rakaia, while narrow-leaved snow tussock is dominant south of the Rakaia and on the flat-topped Central Otago mountains. Broad-leaved snow tussock is widespread on Canterbury mountains. On the wetter main divide you find mid-ribbed snow tussock and the curled snow tussock, and short (fescue) tussock is common in basins such as Mackenzie. The striking and beautiful red tussock was once widespread in Southland but is now found mainly in such places as Mavora Lakes.

Common throughout the beech forest is the mistletoe, particularly in the picnic and camping areas. It's a beech parasite that is easy to spot, with its distinctive leaves giving the game away. In flower the mistletoe is a brilliant red.

For a much longer walk there is the Mavora Walkway. Drive to the North Mavora Lake carpark and follow the rough four-wheel-drive track along the lake edge right out into the tussock grasslands. This marked route follows the wide valleys right through to the Greenstone Track, taking 2-3 days to complete. However, a walk there and back along the lake edge is about 4-5 hours return.

FOVEAUX WALKWAY

Features
Coastal scenery and forest.

Walking time
2-3 hours return.

How to get there
Drive from Invercargill to Bluff township, through to the Stirling Point carpark, signposts and termination of Highway 1. There's a cafe and restaurant (open 7 days) overlooking the carpark.

This walking trail at the bottom of the South Island wanders around the distinctive Bluff peninsula and looks across the fabulously stormy Foveaux Strait. The Maori name for Bluff was Motupohue: 'motu' means island, which the Bluff peninsula very nearly is, and 'pohue' is the giant white convolvulus that grows on the peninsula.

From the carpark the well-graded track edges past the scenic reserve, with its mixed podocarp-hardwood forest of rimu, totara, miro, rata and kamahi, ferns underneath, and black supplejack twisting through the understorey. The distinctive orange papery bark of the fuchsia is well in evidence, with its bell-shaped red flower in spring. Bellbirds, fantails and wood pigeons can often be heard.

It's worth turning up the Glory Track for a 15-minute diversion, to climb into a surprisingly dense forest of broadleaf, kamahi, rata, miro and rimu, where fantails circle as if in some private aerial combat.

Out of the forest you reach the gunpits where there are good views to Dog Island with its 36m-tall stripey lighthouse, the tallest in New Zealand, which was erected in 1865 from rock quarried from the island. The original tower has been strengthened and encased in concrete. The lens weighs 4.5 tonnes and sits in a bath of mercury, and the light is now automated. The island itself is only 11 hectares and barely 15m above sea level at its highest point. It averages only 70-80 days a year *without* rain.

FOVEAUX WALKWAY

0   1 km

Invercargill

carpark

Bluff town

Tiwai Point

Bluff Harbour

Gunpit Road

Bluff Hill 268 m

carpark and lookout

Stirling Point carpark
Highway 1 terminus

Glory Track

N

Foveaux Strait

beacon

Back on the main track the sea batters the large bouldery coastline and on a typical day rain squall fuzzes the horizon, occasionally revealing the offshore islands, sometimes in a dazzling burst of sunlight. Past the navigation light the track emerges onto farmland for its final leg back to Highway 1.

OYSTERS

Poor Captain Cook made two famous errors. He called Banks Peninsula an island (later settlers referred to it as Cook's Mistake) and he missed Foveaux Strait completely and lumped Stewart Island with the South Island. However, what most people know the strait for is what lies underneath it – Bluff oysters.

Oysters are molluscs, like mussels, cockles and whelks. They have no teeth or jaw and eat by filtering microscopic plankton through their gills. Most molluscs possess a muscular foot (like a snail), but since the adult oyster does not move it lacks even this feature. (The larval oyster possesses a foot to enable it to find a suitable site, then the foot withers away.) The oyster is vulnerable to predators such as crabs, starfish and drilling whelks, which bore neat holes through its tough shell. Bluff oysters lie in natural beds in the strait, which the oyster boats dredge up using steel mesh. The fishery is controlled to stop over-fishing and the season restricted. Although the *Bonamia* parasite devastated the oyster beds some years ago, careful management has seen the oysters recover.

People have often doubted the supposed aphrodisiac qualities of oysters, but it is known that oysters contain high levels of zinc, which is thought to play an important part in the good health of a man's prostate. The prostate gland seems to have only one use, to provide a transport fluid for the sperm cells, so perhaps there is something in oysters after all. Bon appetit!

SOUTHLAND'S ESTUARIES

From the top of the Bluff lookout you can see an impressive series of coastal estuaries and inland lagoons that run some 80km from Riverton to Fortrose. Despite drainage and reclamation these huge lagoons attract thousands of migratory waders both from New Zealand and the northern hemisphere, particularly in the peak time of October to March.

Over 80 bird species have been recorded in this coastal habitat, which makes the Southland estuaries one of the top three wading-bird habitats in the South Island. The others are Lake Ellesmere and Farewell Spit.

Awarua Bay for example, which is a 20-minute drive from the Bluff lookout, attracts such diverse overseas species as Siberian tatlers (regular visitors), turnstones (common, with some birds wintering over), greenshanks (occasional), sanderlings (occasional), curlew sandpipers (regular visitors), eastern bar-tailed godwits (abundant, with wintering-over birds), red-necked stints (regular), two types of whimbrel (both very rare) and many others. As well as these foreign imports there are the coastal wading standards such as oystercatchers, white-faced herons, black swans, mallards, terns (at least five species have been spotted), and breeding colonies of black-backed gulls and little shags. The endangered New Zealand dotterel, which breeds on Stewart Island, also visits occasionally.

FIORDLAND

Kidney fern

HIDDEN FALLS

Features
Rainforest, waterfall, bush birds, historic
pack track.

Walking time
3 hours return to the second verandah, 4
hours return to Hidden Falls Hut.

How to get there
From Highway 94, 90km from Te Anau,
turn down the Hollyford Road some 15km
to the carpark and the start of the Hollyford
Track at the road end. There is a shop,
campground and cabins at the Hollyford
Motor Camp operated by Murray Gunn.
Also a museum.

The beauty of this walk is its easy grade. You can meander along an historic pack and
cattle track, through dense rainforest with many impressive individual tree specimens,
and admire the jostling mass of pungas and understorey shrubs as they fight for a place
in the sun. There are muted tree-absorbed sounds of bush birds such as wood pigeons,
bellbirds and fantails, and the urban world seems a long way away.

From the carpark the track plunges immediately into tall podocarp rainforest
and leaves the Hollyford River as it cuts inland past a verandah bolted into the rock
that overlooks a quiet backwater. Then the track stays inland, sometimes close

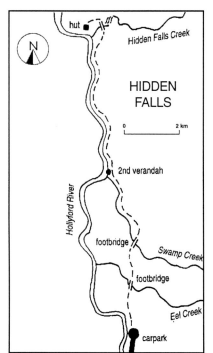

to silent and dry river channels, and
crosses swingbridges over Eel Creek
and Swamp Creek. After 30 minutes it
meets the Hollyford again, and a
second verandah has been cunningly
built out of the cliffside overhanging
the slick dark waters of the river. Five
minutes further on there is the first
decent break in the bush canopy, with
excellent views up to the splinter peaks
of the Darran Mountains, which frequently wear a mask of gloomy cloud.
If you're lucky enough to get a clear
day the mountains are memorable.

This is a good place to start the
return if you do not fancy the longer
hike to Hidden Falls Hut. If you want
to go further, make sure you have
enough time to get back in daylight.

The Hollyford Track sidles along
the riverside for another hour to
Hidden Falls swingbridge and a
glorious view of the thundering falls.

NIC BISHOP

Hidden Falls

There is a large hut a short distance away on the other side of the creek, and quite large grassy and gravel flats afford some previously well-screened views. Mounts Madeleine and Tutoko loom large over the valley and it is surprising to realise that you are barely 100m above sea level, even though it would take you another three days of walking to reach the sea some 60km away.

KEY SUMMIT

Features
Alpine tarns and wetland, beech forest, bog plants, mountain views.

Walking time
2-3 hours return to Key Summit.

How to get there
From Te Anau drive 55km on Highway 94 to the start of the Routeburn Track at the Divide Saddle. Shelter, toilets and carpark.

This small 1000m bump overlooks three crucial river valleys: the Hollyford, the Greenstone and the Eglinton. For all the early travellers in the region – Maori and European – this junction was the key.

The Maori used the Hollyford trail as an important accessway to the greenstone source at the head of Lake Wakatipu, and for the European it was equally important, particularly for the settlement of Jamestown in 1875 at Martins Bay. The lack of success in opening up the Hollyford route was the death-knell for Jamestown. It was also Key Summit that witnessed the early attempts to find an overland route into Milford Sound from the Hollyford Valley, a problem that was not finally solved until the Homer Tunnel was drilled through the hard granite rock of the Darran Mountains.

From the divide carpark the well-graded track (which is of course the start of the western end of Routeburn Track) passes though silver beech forest with ribbonwood and fuchsia. There is a healthy native bird population: riflemen, brown creepers, grey warblers, fantails, bellbirds and tomtits all abound, and there is a reasonable chance of seeing a wood pigeon and hearing a kea, kaka or parakeet.

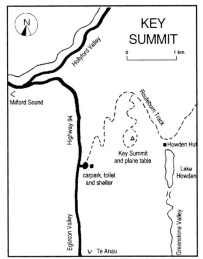

Introduced birds such as chaffinches and blackbirds are common.

From the turnoff to Key Summit the track climbs up through manuka, flax, bog pine and tussock. Key Summit is a long succession of pretty tarns and boglands leading gradually from the bush edge onto the harsher, upper slopes of the Livingstone Mountains. In most seasons this wetland is a multicoloured carpet, with bog cushions, rushes, mosses, alpine sundew, bog pine and many other small herbs and plants. Please take care to keep to the main track as this is a very delicate area.

A small loop track leads around to the first bogland and the mountain-spotting

Tarn on Key Summit

plane table, from where the track continues up a short rise to a second wetland and more good views. From here on the track deteriorates considerably and becomes muddy as it twists in and out of stunted silver beech. Most people probably will not want to bother with this section.

The mountain panorama is breathtaking on a clear day, with the spiky Darran peaks on one side, often snow-covered, contrasting with the softer shapes of the Livingstone Mountains and the Greenstone Valley. The permanence of the mountains is illusory, as the nearby Earl Mountains were, about 200 million years ago, quite close to the South Pole. The molar of Mount Emily is impressive and you can see a bit of Lake Marion as well as following the long, long valley of the Hollyford River.

PIPITS – PIHOIHOI

The New Zealand pipit is arguably this country's most versatile bird. It can be found feeding on insects in tidal pools, or way up high in alpine tussocks, or even above the snowline. Because of this supposed preference for alpine areas, and its resemblance to the song thrush, the early settlers nicknamed it the snow thrush. Its distinctive 'tweeep' and bobbing motion, usually from a handy observation rock, give the pipit a high profile. It would be a desolate place indeed that could not maintain a pair of pipits.

THE CHASM & BOWEN FALLS

Features
Gorge, waterfall, rainforest.

Walking time
The Chasm 20 minutes return, Bowen Falls 20 minutes return.

How to get there
From Te Anau drive 110km to the signposted Chasm Walk, then another 10km on to Milford Sound, where you have to park in the public carpark provided and walk 5 minutes along to the visitor centre and start of the Bowen Falls Track. Petrol, tearooms and shop at Milford, but these are not necessarily open all year round. It might be safer to fill up in Te Anau, as the garage in Milford has been known to run out.

Excellent interpretation signs at the visitor centre and around the foreshore.

These two short walks illustrate the power of Fiordland. The road is almost a wilderness experience in itself, with towering slabs of black mountains, heavy rainforest and the dark, difficult hole of the Homer Tunnel.

Both walks are on the tourist trail and on most summer days you can expect to see buses lined up in ranks at the Chasm and by the Milford Visitor Centre. That's why the carpark at the Chasm is *so* big.

But it is worth noting that as many of the buses come from Queenstown they are on a tight schedule, so day-trippers normally 'do' the Chasm in the morning, drive to Milford Sound, go on a boat trip, and then possibly make a quick trip to Bowen Falls in the afternoon. If you bear this in mind you can plan to arrive at the walks when they are not so busy (early morning or evening are usually good times); Milford can be strangely deserted by 5pm. Remember that if you head to Milford Sound in the afternoon you will certainly encounter buses going the opposite way in the close confines of the Homer Tunnel.

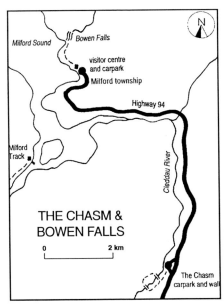

THE CHASM & BOWEN FALLS

The Chasm
The Chasm is a short circuit track around a deep defile where the Cleddau River has ransacked its way through the diorite and in the process created some fantastic and improbable shapes in this most unyielding of rocks. Please keep to

the boardwalked track as the rocks on the side are very slippery. You might be tempted for a better camera angle, but frankly it's almost impossible to get a decent photo of this feature. The river drops abruptly and the heavy rainforest canopy provides such a deep contrast that it defeats every camera, except the human eye. The boardwalk crosses a natural bridge of boulders at one point, and many of the rocks are potholed (moulins) or have had holes bored through them by the relentless pressure of water churning pebbles like small grindstones. After a downpour (not uncommon in these parts) the chasm is like an excited and roaring beast.

Bowen Falls

Bowen Falls is equally spectacular and must be one of the most photographed waterfalls in New Zealand. Unlike at the Chasm, however, here you can get some pretty useful and attractive photographs. The walk is signposted by the visitor centre and follows a boardwalk to the bouldery bank of the 160m falls. It's worth scrambling downriver to the seashore, particularly at low tide, to get good views up and down Milford Sound.

Quite a few shore birds enjoy the estuarine habitat from the falls to Milford township, including the ubiquitous paradise ducks, and the occasional white heron (kotuku) in winter.

Because of the phenomenal rainfall, 6m a year, the seawater sound itself has a 3m layer of fresh water on its surface. This prevents the growth of seaweed, and because this freshwater layer is dark with minute vegetation particles, normally deep-water fauna can exist at a much shallower depth in the sound. The best-known is the black coral, which clings to the steep fiord sides only 5-20m below the surface.

White heron at Milford Sound estuary

LAKE GUNN – O TAPARA

Features
Long-tailed bats, bush lake, yellowheads,
red beech forest.

Walking time
1 hour circuit.

How to get there
From Te Anau drive to the Cascade Creek
campground – some 76km. There are
toilets, picnic tables, campsites and
fireplaces at the camping ground. There is
also a picnic area at the far north end of the
lake, which is usually more sheltered.

The Eglinton Valley is one the best bird-listening posts in the country and one of the few strongholds of the declining yellowhead. Many bird recordings are taken from the Eglinton and you only have to pull off the highway, switch off the engine and open the door to hear what in many regions you have to tramp miles for – tomtits, fantails, parakeets, yellowheads, riflemen, grey warblers, robins, brown creepers, tuis, bellbirds, silvereyes, kakas and wood pigeons, not counting the introduced and vocal blackbirds, song thrushes and sparrows. Their home is the warm, sheltered and moist climate of a forest dominated by red beech, the tallest reaching 30m at an age of 400-500 years.

Lake Gunn is a perfect place to appreciate the tranquillity and maturity of this forest. From the carpark take the first right-hand fork as it plunges into a magic and mysterious grotto of huge buttressed red beech trees, swathed at their bases in a

Forest walk in the Eglinton Valley

155

deep dark moss underworld. The silence can be foreboding. This is forest at its supreme best, with every possible niche occupied by plants. Even the fallen trees seem to have attained a profound dignity of purpose. Silver beech, lancewood and broadleaf are common understorey trees.

Closer to the 3km-long lake, fluctuating water levels stop the larger trees from gaining a foothold and more adaptable manuka and flax become common. The lake can often be mirror-calm, with the surface occasionally broken by brown and rainbow trout as well as Atlantic salmon. Bird sounds seem deceptively close.

The track rejoins the main path and there is a short side-track to the shyer, shallower Black Lake, which can freeze over in winter and offers some of the best views and reflections of the surrounding Livingstone Mountains. The tussock 'bridge' is an excellent picnic and musing spot. Follow the main track alongside the river to the camping and picnic area, then the road back to the carpark.

LONG-TAILED BATS – PEKAPEKA

Long-tailed bats have been the subject of an extensive study in the Eglinton and Hollyford valleys. They are born fliers, much more so than their rarer cousins the short-tailed bats. The long-tails have a body about the size of a human thumb, weigh about 7-12g and have a wingspan of up to 20cm. Their lifespan is still something of a mystery but they feed mostly on insects and live both in small colonies and in individual roosts, usually preferring old established trees. They are most active in the summer months, when insects abound. At cold temperatures they stay inactive (torpid), though whether they actually hibernate is not known.

The long-tailed bat is the commoner of the two bat species and has been reported from a wide number of sites around New Zealand, from Northland to Stewart Island. It seems to be suffering a decline, perhaps through predation or habitat loss, and in some places where it has been recorded regularly before, such as Banks Peninsula, there have been no recent sightings at all.

The best time to see the long-tails is at dusk, and Lake Gunn is a good place to catch them flitting like nervous turbo-propelled swallows. There are no swallows in the Eglinton or Hollyford valleys, so if you think you've seen a swallow, you've seen a bat!

SHALLOW BAY

Features
Sphagnum moss swamp, bush birds, beech forest, lake, dragonflies.

Walking time
2-3 hours return to Shallow Beach.

How to get there
On the road between Te Anau and Manapouri townships drive about 12km south from Te Anau to the Rainbow Reach carpark and footbridge. This is also one end of the Kepler Track.

Manapouri is the fifth-largest lake in New Zealand and the Maori originally called it Rotoua (the rainy lake) and Moturau (many islands). The eastern end of the lake was a favoured food-gathering area for the Maori and evidence of occupation has been found at most inlets, beaches and islands.

A plan to raise the lake level in the 1960s for more hydro-electric power caused a huge public uproar and a petition of 265,000 signatures succeeded in defeating the plan. The lake has a degree of enchantment about it: it is not as big or hostile as Lake Te Anau, and mists frequently blur its distinction from the mountains.

From the Rainbow Reach carpark the track (which is the main Kepler Track) crosses the swingbridge and follows the Waiau River downstream in the fertile river terraces. Red and mountain beech and a thick carpet of crown ferns make up the forest here, as the track wanders around Balloon Loop, a side channel of the Waiau. The moss is lush, like green fur – you are tempted to stroke it.

The track crosses a swingbridge over the Forest Burn and climbs slightly to an attractive sphagnum moss swamp and lookout platform on the lake. This 'kettle lake' was formed when a large block of ice from a glacier was isolated and trapped on the glacial moraine. Rich peat deposits of decomposed material form a low-oxygen environment that is ideal for many plants and animals, including the sphagum moss.

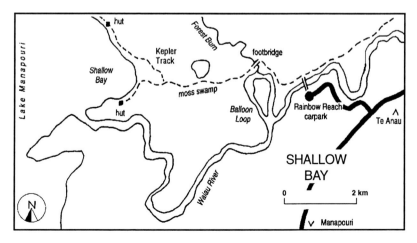

157

Scaup

Around the edge of the clearing are tall podocarps: pure stands of kahikatea grow on swampy ground and other podocarps – miro, matai and rimu – are common. Orchids enjoy this type of mixed wetland habitat, but not as much as the invertebrates like mayflies and dragonflies – it's a piece of dragonfly heaven.

After the moss swamp the track reaches a signposted junction from where the Shallow Bay Track drops down to the lakeside and follows the gravel beach to the quiet six-bunk hut. Bush birds can be plentiful: tuis, bellbirds, riflemen, grey warblers, fantails, tomtits, wood pigeons, fernbirds, parakeets and yellowheads are often heard and frequently seen. On the lake there are paradise ducks, grey ducks and scaup. Introduced mallard ducks and Canada geese visit during the winter.

SPHAGNUM MOSS

This is an interesting example of a plant once thought useless and now so highly valued that there have been instances of sphagnum poaching! The quality that makes sphagnum so valuable is its ability to absorb up to 20 times its own weight in water. This makes it ideal as a potting medium and exports to Japan, mainly for the orchid market, are over 700 tonnes a year – $10 million worth. Because sphagnum moss is sterile and harbours no bacteria, it was used for bandages in World War I and has now found a modern use in sanitary pads. Sphagnum has no root system and can be easily picked. There are a number of sphagnum species, and texture and colour can vary widely.

STEWART ISLAND

Fuchsia

MAORI BEACH

Features
Coastal forest, sandy beaches, bush birds.

Walking time
3-4 hours return to Maori Beach.

How to get there
There are two routes to Stewart Island: a 20-minute hop by air or the catamaran Foveaux Express, which takes about an hour to cross the wild strait. Both services operate all year round, though with reduced services during the winter months. There is plenty of accommodation at Oban (including backpackers) and all facilities.
From Oban walk over to Horseshoe Bay, then take the road to Lee Bay to the start of the Rakiura Track (5km).

Rakiura (land of the glowing skies) is a more poetic and apt name for this wilderness island. William Stewart was the first officer on board the ship *Pegasus*, which landed in the southern harbour in 1809, and left behind his prosaic name on this lovely isle.

This far south the skies have a soft elusive light, constantly changing as rain squalls drift across the low, thickly forested island. You can receive the full range of weather on a single day, from heavy rain to bright sunshine and then more rain. It is a mild, moist maritime climate and there is virtually no such thing as a dry season.

It is undoubtedly one of the best places in New Zealand to see native birds. You don't even have to leave Oban to see any number of fat wood pigeons precariously perched on the telephone wires. Tuis scuffle among the township's trees and parakeets

Tui

161

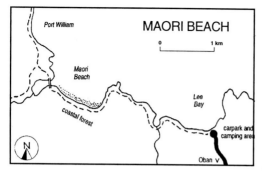

MAORI BEACH

0   1 km

Port William

Maori Beach

coastal forest

Lee Bay

carpark and camping area

Oban

keep up a constant background chatter. The birdlife is prolific on Rakiura and markedly friendlier. Any visitor who gets a little away from Oban will see and hear good numbers of kakas, and maybe – just maybe – even a kiwi.

The track to Maori Beach starts from Lee Bay and is also the start of the Rakiura Track. There is plenty of Stewart Island mud but the track is well graded as it was once the main route to the sawmill settlement at Maori Beach. There is a campsite at Lee Bay.

The forest is initially cutover, with fuchsia and supplejack. Then kamahi and rimu start to dominate, with some tall rimu closer to Maori Beach. Southern rata is particularly evident around the pretty Little River estuary. Beech forest is absent, though it was once present. A glacial period 10,000 years ago swept the island clear of forest and the bird-dispersed podocarp seeds quickly returned, but the slower 'creeping' dispersal methods of beech forest have not allowed it to return.

It's about 30 minutes to Little River and the track skirts the sand at low tide. Upstream from the bridge there is a pleasant picnic and camping site with a toilet, and some splendid rata and rimu trees. The track climbs steeply and glimpses the bouldery coastline as it wanders across the headland at Peters Point and drops abruptly to Maori Beach. At a lower tide you can cross directly to the beach but there is a (very muddy) high-tide alternative track if you get stuck.

Maori Beach is a 1km sweep of sand – golden when the elusive Stewart Island sun emerges. There is a designated camping area at the east end, with cooking shelter and toilet. On one tree at the campsite there is a huge cascading tree orchid, which is a trifle disconcerting for those who think orchids are shy reclusive plants. It's worthwhile visiting the old sawmill remains, where a massive boiler broods in silence.

Those with more energy and time can go on to Port William, but the track from Maori beach does a big 150m up-and-down climb before dropping to Magnetic Beach. In the 1870s Port William was the site of a government-sponsored settlement, mainly of hardy Shetland Islanders. Tough they may have been, but limited access to markets crippled the settlement and the gum trees are a reminder of this dogged attempt. There is a hut, jetty, picnic and camping areas.

162